A GODDESS
AMONG US

THE DIVINE LIFE OF
ANANDAMAYI MA

Swami Mangalananda

YogiImpressions®

YogiImpressions®

A GODDESS AMONG US
First published in India in 2007 by
Yogi Impressions Books Pvt. Ltd.
1711, Centre 1, World Trade Centre,
Cuffe Parade, Mumbai 400 005, India.
Website: www.yogiimpressions.com

First Edition: June 2007
Revised Edition: April 2009
Fifth reprint: November 2015

Cover concept, design and edited by Shiv Sharma
Photos courtesy: Richard Lannoy and Ashram Archives

ISBN 978-81-88479-45-0

Printed at: Repro India Ltd., Mumbai

"For one who knows me,
I am one with him;
for one who wants to know me,
I am very near to him;
and for one who does not know me,
I am a beggar before him."

– Anandamayi Ma

CONTENTS

FOREWORD

Who is Anandamayi Ma, and how do we write about her? Ma is the Mother of All.

For six consecutive years (1976-1982), I lived and moved in Ma's Presence. During this entire period, there was not a single moment when I perceived Ma as a simple human being, but always beheld her as a living, human manifestation of complete and perfect divinity.

An American disciple of Ma, Swami Mangalananda has lived in our ashram in India for many years. He has performed an invaluable service in writing this brief and readable account of the events of Ma's life.

Ma's spiritual message is that: 'All is One; we have gathered here on earth not to quarrel, but to make the best use of our existence, to make our lives meaningful by realising Truth.'

By reading the pages of this book, you will not be reading the life of a historical character alien to yourself, but you will have literally begun the discovery of your own deeper self. When you finish this book, you will undoubtedly feel an unknown urge arising from the innermost recesses of your heart to be one with Ma. This will lead you to your real destiny and be a lamp shining on your path to the fulfillment of the very purpose of the evolutionary process. At its conclusion, it will be seen that the path, the struggle, and the goal are all none other than Ma herself, the Divine Supreme.

Jai Ma!

— Swami Kedarnath
Mata Anandamayi Tapo Bhumi,
Omkareshwar,
Madhya Pradesh, India.

PREFACE

There are many authoritative and well-written books about the life and teachings of Anandamayi Ma. But, all the existing books are rather voluminous and are available only from a limited number of sources.

What was lacking was a brief biography that included the high points of Ma's life, with a few suitable pictures. Such a book could be priced fairly, distributed widely, read quickly, and would, hopefully, serve to acquaint people with the divine life of Anandamayi Ma. If anyone wanted to know more, there was always the standard literature one could acquire. It is hoped that this short biography, written specifically at the request of the devotees of our ashram, will fulfill this need.

To some extent, almost all biographies reflect the subjective views of the author, and this book is certainly no exception.

It is not meant to be a reference book, but an informal introduction to a divine and inspiring life that should never be forgotten.

Although the life of Anandamayi Ma is filled with supernatural and miraculous events, it is not the life of a legendary figure of some bygone era, embellished with fanciful folk tales handed down from generation to generation. Many people living today, including the author, witnessed the events recounted in the books written on her life. Most of these are drawn from the personal accounts of friends, relatives and other witnesses who experienced these incidents and occurrences for themselves. May all who had the grace of meeting Ma, continue doing everything possible to keep her memory alive and teachings relevant for succeeding generations, so that this unique entity who came among us, may continue to influence and uplift the human race.

— Swami Mangalananda
Mata Anandamayi Tapo Bhumi,
Omkareshwar,
Madhya Pradesh, India.

INTRODUCTION

Throughout the history of humankind, great saints and sages have come to spread the light of spirituality in a darkened world. In India, it is believed that God Himself has incarnated or appeared many times to restore victory of good over evil, re-establish the Path of Righteousness, and guide humanity to the revelation of its innate divinity.

Anandamayi Ma was often asked the pertinent question, "Who are you?" She would reply to this question, at different times, in different ways. She once told a very close disciple, *"I am the vyakta rupa of the pure aspiration of all true spiritual aspirants. You called for this body, and now you have it among you."* By this definition, we see that Ma belongs to all who feel an inner yearning for the Divine, and she came for all of us. To know and study her life is of great importance and significance.

Many times, Ma stressed that the manifestation of her birth was not a result of *karma*, as is the case of a soul trapped in relativity. We are bound by our karma and by the destiny we have to fulfill. Ma was a completely 'free' being, and her every action and word was an expression of this freedom and divinity. Therefore, every minute detail of her life bears a moral lesson. Those who saw her felt that every movement of her body was a divine expression of sublime beauty and grace.

Ma frequently said that everything she did was for all of us. The *lila* that she performed on the world stage was for all those who had joined their minds and hearts to hers. She became a repository of all spiritual blessings and powers, and still is, to those who know of her and think of her.

Ma also said that no one could think of her unless she first thinks of them. Therefore, in the knowing of her life, and in thinking of her divine lila, we tune in to all her virtues and perfection for the blessing and upliftment of our own hearts and lives. The more we know about her life and teachings, the more that eternal life lives in us, and her words can constantly guide our actions in the difficult times we live in.

Anandamayi as the young Nirmala Sundari Devi

A DIVINE
CHILD

On 30th April, 1896, a beautiful girl-child was born at Kheora village, in the Tripura district of East Bengal (now Bangladesh). Her family traced its descent from *Rishi* Kashyapa, who was a devout worshipper of Lord Vishnu. Her mother, Mokshada Sundari Devi, the embodiment of simple and pure virtues, would play an important role in the child's later manifestation as *Ma*. She was affectionately addressed as *Didima*. Before the birth of this child, she had many visions of gods, goddesses, and the divine light that entered into her.

The child's father, Bipin Bihari Bhattacharya, was a very religious and otherworldly man, who spent his days singing the praises of God in a sweet, soul-stirring voice. Sometimes, he would stay absent for months at a time, wandering as a penniless mendicant, singing *bhajans* and practicing spiritual discipline.

The child was named Nirmala Sundari Devi, which means 'goddess of flawless beauty'. In later years, Ma always stressed that she has always been the same. *"As I was at birth, and as a child, so am I now."* Didima said that at birth she never uttered a cry, but was very peaceful, radiant and possessed full consciousness. She later amazed people by recalling the names of those who were present at her birth, and of events that occurred in her early years.

The first sign that her mother had of her supernatural identity came when the child was just a few months old. One day, as Nirmala lay in her crib and Didima was going about her household chores, she noticed that a *sadhu* with a radiant face and long, matted locks was standing before the crib with folded hands. He addressed the mother and said, "This is no ordinary child, and she will not be confined within an ordinary life. This is none other than the 'Mother' of the whole world!" After giving his blessing he walked out of the door and when Didima looked out after him, he was nowhere to be seen.

The small child grew into a sweet-natured and friendly little girl. The second dominant trait in her life was also noticed during childhood. She never had a desire of her own or moved to fulfill any personal wish. If left to herself, she reposed blissfully contented in her own self. What motivated all her actions and movements during childhood and throughout her life, were the desires and needs of others. It was seen that the young Nirmala was always at hand to serve and help others. Transcending all social and caste barriers, she was loved by everyone in the village.

The child's favourite playmate was her grandmother, known affectionately as *Thakurma*. This elderly lady would occasionally be surprised when the little girl would, with scholarly precision, correct the Sanskrit in a *sloka* that she was reciting. On one occasion, little Nirmala showed Thakurma the correct and intricate *mudras* to be perform during puja. Another time, while the two were playing together, Thakurma, after an intense and penetrating look from young Nirmala, went into a deep, inner state of *samadhi*.

At the age of four, Nirmala was taken to a *kirtan* in the village. During the chanting of the holy names, she became so engrossed in a deep inner *bhav*, that tears started streaming from her eyes.

AN UNCOMMON
GIRL

Always happy and laughing, Nirmala grew into a young girl, with the trees and plants, the sunshine and the open air as her playmates. Unaffected by heat or cold, she would play in the hot sun, and sing and dance in the rain. She was frequently seen talking to plants and animals, and to entities visible only to herself. As she and some girls from the village were returning from the forest one afternoon, they were confronted by a herd of cows blocking the road ahead. As her scared companions scurried up a hill to bypass the herd, they looked down and saw that all the cows had surrounded Nirmala, and were affectionately licking her hands and touching their heads to her feet.

Her mother grew concerned that perhaps her young daughter was somewhat mentally retarded, for she frequently manifested states of complete inner absorption and abstraction. Didima, not realising that this was a manifestation of the highest states of *yogic* samadhi, mistook this for absent-mindedness or some illness. Sometimes, while she was eating, Nirmala's hand would freeze midway and she would remain still, staring up into the sky. Years later, when Didima asked her about this, Ma laughingly replied that she was watching the gods and goddesses passing in procession in the sky, before her inner gaze.

At every stage of life, Nirmala manifested the ideal fulfillment of that stage of human *dharma*. As a child, she was sweet and selfless. As she grew into a young girl, she manifested every virtue natural to that age. She was totally obedient to her parents and teachers, and naturally shunned any form of dishonesty or cunning. On one occasion, while visiting a neighbouring village with relatives, she was told to wait outside the temple while the women went for some shopping in the local bazaar. After shopping for several hours, the women suddenly remembered little Nirmala and rushed back to the spot, expecting to find her gone. But, on arriving, they found her sitting in the exact position and spot that they had left her in. She had sat unmoving, in perfect obedience to that simple command, for hours!

Nirmala was drawn to all religious observances, and was loved by the Muslims as much as by the Hindus of the village. One night, she secretly left the house to watch a camp meeting being held by a group of visiting Christian missionaries and to listen to their hymns. She loved to spend her evening hours singing religious bhajans with her father.

A carefree girl, Nirmala would often amaze her playmates and elders with her profound knowledge and wisdom. Once, when playing in a pile of sand, she made a perfectly round ball from the wet sand. Holding it up in her hand, she said, *"As Narayana is present in the Shaligram, so do I see all devas and forms in this. All is in One,* and *the One is in all."* So saying, she broke the ball and merrily went her way.

Sometimes, while playing, she would suddenly become still and indrawn, and her face would shine with a luminosity that was described by onlookers as 'a play of lightning across the sky.' At times, when she was in this state, holy *mantras* would issue from her mouth in immaculate Sanskrit.

At this stage of her life, young Nirmala not only went to school, but she also learned all the household skills required of a young Indian girl, and excelled in sewing and cooking. Although she was of a sweet temperament and gentle behaviour, her elders came to realise that she was a power not to be trifled with. Once when she was asked to fill a pot with curds and bring it into the kitchen, it was seen that she had obediently filled the pot brimful, leaving no space at the top. "Foolish girl!" she was admonished, "You will get no curd for yourself today!" Suddenly, at these words, the pot, which was across the room, cracked apart, spilling the curd all over the floor.

Young Nirmala with her parents Bipin Bhattacharya and Mokshada Devi

A BRIDE
AT THIRTEEN

According to the prevalent custom of the day, Nirmala's marriage was arranged when she was still very young. A boy from a *Brahmin* family living in the nearby village of Atpara, was found to be a suitable match, and after all the formalities were completed, a date was set for the marriage ceremony. The marriage took place on 7th February, 1909, when Nirmala was thirteen years old. Her husband, Ramani Mohan Chakravarty, was considerably older than her and was working in the police force.

Immediately after the wedding, she returned with her parents to her village. She would only go to live with her husband after several years. Almost two years later, while Ramani was stationed elsewhere, Nirmala was sent to live with her husband's family.

In her new surroundings, Nirmala displayed a perfection and grace of conduct perfectly suited to her circumstances.

She became the embodiment of the perfect housewife. Usually keeping her face covered in a *ghunghat*, she showed respect and humility before her elders, and devoted herself to performing household duties. The family soon came to love and cherish this modest, sweet-tempered girl who appeared to be skilled in every household craft. She was so uncomplaining, good-natured and constantly doing household chores that her hands became cracked and bled from the excessive work. The family soon realised how hard she was applying herself to please them.

The children of the household adored her and were heard saying that they felt like calling her 'Ma' rather than Aunty. She soon became known for her culinary skills. She was once told that a certain visitor, who was coming to dinner that evening, abhorred radish and couldn't stand even the sight of that vegetable in any dish. Nirmala laboured all day over the preparation of the food. After the meal was over, the guest was enthusiastically proclaiming how he had enjoyed it. Laughingly, Nirmala then revealed that the entire meal, including the dessert, was made entirely of radish prepared in several different ways.

In 1914, when Nirmala was eighteen years old, her husband, who was then living in Ashtagram, called for her to come and join him. Before she left, Didima told her daughter to obey her husband as her *guru*, in the same way as she had obeyed and honoured them. Nirmala took this piece of good advice to heart, and it became the keystone of her new and unusual relationship with her husband throughout their married life.

So far, Ramani had thought he had married a simple village girl and had received reports that she was very hardworking and was pleasant-natured. When she entered his life, he found her to be so holy, otherworldly, and surrounded with such an intense spiritual aura, that any thought of a normal married life was driven from his mind. In truth, the man destined to be her husband and guardian was a rare personality, well suited for this profound responsibility. In later years, Ma said that he never had a carnal thought or impulse cross his conscious mind, and on the rare occasion that she felt a slight impulse arise undetected from deep within his subconscious mind, she would immediately enter into deep samadhi. Becoming alarmed, he would start doing kirtan and recite mantras to bring her back to outer consciousness, thus completely clearing his mind. Towards his last days, he witnessed that Ma was an *Akhanda Brahmacharini* or *Sanatan Kumari*.

Ramani came to look upon his wife as a Divine Child, and himself as her guardian. He later looked to her for spiritual guidance as his guru. Ma was, at all times, loving, respectful, and obedient to him, and always asked his permission before going anywhere or starting any endeavour. Observing her simple and childlike temperament, he would often say, "That's alright, you are young now. You will think differently when you grow up." In later years, Ma would relate this and laughingly exclaim, *"It seems I never grew up!"*

Once again, Nirmala entered fully into this new life, manifesting a perfect bhava and fulfilling all her duties with customary ease. She served her husband faultlessly, looking after his every comfort, displaying her domestic talents and skills.

Her appearance at this time was also striking. She was slim and graceful, her long, black hair hung below her knees, and her tangible spiritual radiance evoked awe in all who saw her. Once, the new couple was invited to attend a celebration of *Durga Puja*. When Ma, who at that time was unknown to the local people, entered the gathering wearing a red *saree*, the people assembled there were awestruck and proclaimed, "Durga Herself has come into our midst," and began making obeisance, by kneeling and touching their heads to the ground.

She soon became known as *Ranga Didi* and witnesses declared that when she came to the river bank, the area was lit up by her radiant, unearthly beauty. They observed that when she walked at night without a lantern, her body would be enveloped by a soft glow.

At this time, a neighbour by the name of Hara Kumar Rai became the first person to address her as 'Ma'. He was of a devout, religious nature, and would approach her to take *prasad* from her hands. Nirmala, who always maintained the strictest decorum, only consented after obtaining her husband's permission. Hara Kumar Rai made the prophetic statement, "Now, only I address you as 'Ma', but someday the whole world will call you such."

THE MANIFESTATION
OF 'MA'

Here in Ashtagram, Ma first manifested unearthly bhavas during a kirtan organised by some neighbours. As the men sang to the accompaniment of drums and hand cymbals, the women watched from separate quarters at some distance. Suddenly, Ma's body was drawn up like a dry leaf in the wind and, barely touching the ground, she floated into the midst of the kirtan gathering. Exhibiting all the signs of *Mahabhav*, a highly-charged spiritual emotion arising from an intense love for God, Ma's body was alternately floating and rolling on the ground to the rhythm of the music, her eyes and face bathed in a radiant glow. Finally, she sank to the ground and entered into a deep trance. After she remained in this state for a long time, the kirtan had to be resumed to bring her back to normal consciousness.

In 1918, Ramani was posted as an estate clerk at Bajitpur, near Dhaka. It was now that the most intense and esoteric stage of Ma's life began and, perhaps, this phase of her life is of the deepest significance for all *sadhakas*.

Ma frequently used the word *kheyal* to describe the inspiration for her actions. The word loosely implies a mood or frame of mind. Ma used it to denote an 'inner movement of Divine Will' which then took expression in thought or speech. Since Ma was 'Pure Consciousness' and had no 'mind' in the form of conscious or subconscious conditioning, divine inspiration and desire alone expressed itself through what we call 'thought' in her mind. It was this alone that motivated her speech and movements.

Ma describes the beginning of this next phase of her life in this way:

One morning as she was bathing in the pond at Bajitpur, she felt a kheyal arising in her mind: *'What would it be like to play the part of a sadhaka?'* With that inner movement of thought, Ma described that the integral and perfect knowledge of Reality, which had been with her since birth, had a slight veil drawn over it, simply to see how it would be pierced. Hence the lila of *sadhana* began, and continued with intensity for the next six years. As in every phase of Ma's life, she herself did nothing willfully, but everything manifested spontaneously and effortlessly.

Every evening, after completing her household duties, Ma took her husband's permission to practice spiritual disciplines. She would clean a section of the room where she slept and after lighting incense, would sit silently in *yogasana*. Then, quietly repeating *Hari*, the name of God, she would enter into a deep state of meditation. Every night, her husband would curiously observe her, until sleep overtook him. He observed how various yogic *asanas* and *kriyas* would spontaneously and gracefully manifest in her body. At one point he asked her, "We are *Shaktas*, so why are you saying the name of Hari?" Ma replied, *"Then should I say 'Jai Shiva Shankara'?"* He agreed, and Ma continued with this name. The yogic manifestations continued to unfold whenever she was repeating that name, illustrating the point that all the divine names are equally potent.

In later years, Ma would advise that if spiritual practice was applied and continued, everything that was needed would manifest at the proper time. She would also say that any divine name that appeals to a person should be repeated regularly and, if the practice was sincere and steady, God, when necessary, would send anything else that was needed. Ma gave a powerful demonstration of this principle. She began her practice of repeating the name of Shiva. She described how this practice brought deep divine states, how the name became linked with the breath, and the various changes it produced in her consciousness. The asanas and kriyas that were needed to support this practice, spontaneously manifested in her mind and body at the required time.

Anandamayi during her early years at Bajitpur

Anandamayi with her husband Ramani Mohan Chakravarty

SELF-INITIATION
BY MA

Ma said that when the time is right for the disciple, the guru would make an appearance to impart the necessary knowledge and guidance to continue on the Godward path. She stressed that although the guru appears outwardly in different forms, the guru is only One – God Himself as the In-dweller of the heart. In Ma's case, everything manifested naturally from within to illustrate these points. Therefore, after about two years of intense *japa sadhana*, her initiation from the guru took place in a unique way.

On 3rd August, 1922, the auspicious night of *Rakhi Purnima*, Ma spontaneously drew a *yantra* on the floor where she was sitting, and all the steps of *Guru Diksha* were spontaneously revealed in the exact pattern as prescribed in the *shastras*. Later, Ma described how everything that was needed, including the vessels for the worship, offerings etc., were brought forth from within her own self, in subtle form.

Then, in a mysterious way, the guru himself appeared from within her, imparted the mantra and the empowerment, and was absorbed back within her. Her husband woke up in the morning to find her counting the *japa* of this mantra on her fingers, as is shown during the initiation.

From this point on, her sadhana became even more intense. Ma said that although she had described much of all that occurred during this period, only one-thousandth of what occurred has been made known. She spontaneously manifested every possible sadhana and practice known to humankind, not only in Hindu tradition, but also in other religious faiths and traditions. Practices that take aspirants lifetimes to perfect, were manifested through her body in a matter of minutes, and taken to their complete fulfillment. In later years, when people from all over the world, and from every different spiritual background and lineage, came to Ma for advice, she instantly knew every intricate detail of whatever practice they were engaged in, and gave detailed instruction for its correct practice.

Ma said, *"Whatever happened was for all of you only."* As such, in Ma's own person, we find the embodiment of all sadhana and *sadhana shakti.* She would say that all paths to God are her paths. Ma became the patron of all sincere spiritual aspirants.

During this period, an important event occurred where Ma first revealed her true identity. Two of her relatives who were visiting, on seeing Ma engaged in yogic practices in an inner room, asked her husband why she was behaving in such a strange manner. They then approached and told her that to do these practices required initiation from a guru. Ma replied that this initiation had already taken place. They then asked if her husband had received *diksha*. She said, not as yet, but then named the auspicious date, along with the astrological settings, when this would take place. They then chastised her for her seemingly strange behaviour. Suddenly, Ma manifested a powerful and luminous countenance and bhav, and the visitors drew back in amazement. They then asked her plainly, "Who are you?" She first replied, *"I am both Mahadeva and Mahadevi."* They inquired further, and Ma uttered the words *"Purna Brahma Narayana."* They asked for a demonstration of her power. Calling her husband, she placed her hand on his head and he immediately entered a deep state of yogic samadhi and remained entranced for a long time. On being called again to outer consciousness, he confided that he had experienced a state of bliss and consciousness that was beyond description. All these facts were kept secret by the family for many years, until they became spontaneously revealed at a later date.

In January 1923, the day that Ma had predicted for her husband's diksha arrived. Knowing that he left early for work without having breakfast, thus unknowingly fulfilling the condition of the disciple's fasting before the initiation, Ma sent word that he should return or she herself would come for him. Fearing a scene, he returned home to find everything in readiness for the ceremony. Ma gave him a clean towel and asked him to bathe. Then, with great power and authority, the entire ceremony of empowerment and instruction poured forth spontaneously from her lips. The holy mantra was imparted and as he began to repeat it, he was drawn into a deep and blissful state of concentration. Although somewhat unwillingly at first, but from then on with great enthusiasm and energy, Ramani entered the spiritual phase of his life. Ma then gave him the name of *Bholanath* – a name of Shiva denoting His gentle and natural temperament. As the story of Ma's life unfolds, we also observe Bholanath's nature being moulded and transmuted from a simple and mundane, though virtuous, man of the world – into a great sadhu, *sanyasi* and rishi. He became the guiding father of the family of devotees that would eventually gather around Ma.

After six years of an intense manifestation of sadhana and *tapasya*, Ma had the all-encompassing vision of herself manifesting as the entire Universe, and once again the self-imposed veil that had temporarily obscured the perfect Reality, was forever rent in two. Ma then entered a three-year period of complete silence and withdrawal into herself.

BEES TO
THE LOTUS

The year 1924 is regarded by Ma's devotees as perhaps the most memorable, for it was now that the nectar of Ma's divine presence began to draw devotees to her as bees to the lotus. She began to manifest as the Blissful Mother among her children. It all started when Bholanath and Ma moved to Dhaka, the capital of modern-day Bangladesh. Initially, Bholanath was unable to find employment and was thinking of returning to the countryside, but Ma, who was still observing *maun*, made a gesture indicating that he should wait for three more days. Bholanath secured a position, within three days, as Manager of the estate of the *Nawab* of Dhaka. He was given the charge of a large garden estate called Shahbagh, a beautiful and densely wooded area with lakes and gardens. The couple was given a small cottage to live in. As Ma was still completely withdrawn into herself, Bholanath asked some family members to live with them to take care of the house and look after Ma. Eventually, Ma's parents moved in with them, thus setting the stage for the unfolding of the next phase of Ma's lila.

One rainy morning, as Bholanath was standing at the gates of the estate, a man by the name of Prangopal Mukerji was walking by without an umbrella. Bholanath invited him to come in and take shelter until the showers passed. The man gratefully accepted and soon they entered into casual conversation. After some time, Bholanath confessed his worries to the stranger. He told him how very concerned he was about his beloved wife. "She is so inwardly drawn," he said, "I can't understand her, and the mere mention of the name of God sends her into strange mystical states." Prangopal Mukerji was a highly-placed and influential man in local society, and also a great devotee of God, with interest in all things spiritual. Bholanath's statement immediately drew his interest, and he asked if he could meet with Bholanath's wife. He was taken into the presence of Ma, who spent most of her time immersed in samadhi in one of the inner rooms. Mukerji was overwhelmed by the divine radiance of Ma's presence, and upon leaving remarked to Bholanath not to worry. His wife's condition was not a result of illness, but a manifestation of supreme holiness. He then began to spread the word to his friends that there was a *Mataji* living in the Shahbagh Gardens who was immersed in a God-conscious state. Soon, the local people began to come regularly and simply sit quietly in her presence, as she was still observing silence.

Eventually, her silence was lifted and she once again began to speak. By now, a regular group of visitors had formed, and as the annual celebration of *Kali Puja* was approaching, they requested Bholanath, who was a Brahmin priest by caste and occupation, to celebrate the puja at Shahbagh in Ma's presence. He agreed, and on the evening of the festival, they all beseeched Ma to initiate the puja.

Ma began offering flowers to the goddess Kali, but quickly entered into a deep bhav and completely identifying herself with the goddess, began placing flowers on her own head as well. Everyone was overwhelmed with the brilliance of her countenance, and many people had visions of her as Kali. This would be remembered as the first public appearance of Ma. Bholanath, being of a friendly and affable nature, didn't mind the influx of visitors into the estate and always took part in the festivities. Ma cautioned him that if this went on and the doors were flung open to the world, there would then be no possibility of turning back and stemming the flow. However, he had no reservations about sharing Ma's blossoming spiritual manifestation with the whole of humankind, and lovingly welcomed every newcomer.

THREE BELOVED
DEVOTEES

After the Kali Puja, Ma's fame spread by word-of-mouth, and the devotees began to gather in large numbers. Many of them remained faithful to her for the rest of their lives. The most distinct among the devotees were three persons who would become Ma's trusted companions. The man who became known as the most perfect devotee of Ma, and was known to all simply as *Bhaiji*, was Jyotish Chandra Roy. He was the assistant to the District Minister of Agriculture, and had a wife and family. Educated and westernised, he had a rational and enquiring mind. Ma also opened up the fountain of devotion within him, and led him into a life of sadhana and earnest spiritual striving with complete faith in her guidance.

The second remarkable devotee was Shashanka Mohan Mukerjee, a distinguished civil surgeon and social leader. He became totally dedicated to Ma and spent the rest of his life in her company. The third devotee was his daughter, Adorini Devi, who was given the name Gurupriya Devi by Ma, and she was known to all simply as *Didi*. She became Ma's inseparable companion and attendant, and was loved by all the devotees. After years of keeping a daily diary of her experiences with Ma, and of Ma's daily interaction with people, she was persuaded to publish the invaluable manuscript, which today provides us with priceless information about Ma's life and lila.

What did people see in Ma that so captivated their hearts? They found a combination of the sweetness of maternal affection and the profound depths of a mystical knower of God. In this fragile, delicate, young woman, they found the strength and energy of the *Devi* Herself, together with the concern and care of an old and trusted friend. Her sweet smile held everyone spellbound and, as all who have seen Ma can testify, there was the profound sense of knowing her at a deep and eternal level, and a sense of being known by her from all eternity. Those who had met her just hours earlier, felt as if they were meeting their very own after a long absence and were reluctant to leave her presence.

Even people who were not interested in religion and spirituality were attracted to Ma, and she awakened a deep spiritual longing in a completely natural and spontaneous manner in everyone. In the Shahbagh Gardens, the sounds of kirtan, puja, discourses and general merriment resounded day and night. Many people were so reluctant to leave that they even spread their blankets in the hall near Ma, and late at night slept at her feet, so they could see her again first thing in the morning. Meals were cooked and eaten in common, Ma herself frequently helping with the preparation and serving.

Each person received spiritual instruction and guidance according to his or her temperament and *samskara*. Ma became known as *Manusha Kali* and also as the 'Ma of Shahbagh Gardens'.

Seeing Ma's complete even-mindedness and indifference to her own comfort, Bholanath once asked, half-jokingly, if she could eat some raw chilli powder that he was using in the cooking. Ma calmly took a handful of the flaming red powder, put it into her mouth and swallowed it. Her smiling countenance remained unmoved as Bholanath watched in amazement. Afterwards, he himself fell ill with acute dysentery and stomach pains. As Ma lovingly nursed him to recovery, she solemnly told him, *"I have told you never to test me like this."* The lesson was learned.

In the early days, Bhaiji's keen and rational mind was continually putting Ma to the test. He once asked her if, being beyond bodily sensation, she could put a burning coal on her foot without feeling any pain. Ma simply laughed, but then, when Bhaiji was not looking, placed a burning coal on top of her foot, and calmly watched as it slowly burned a deep hole in her foot. Afterwards, she explained that the kheyal arose to simply witness the fun. Bhaiji was struck dumb with remorse at his foolish request, and it was only his devotion that compelled Ma to heal her foot.

TRANSFORMATION
DURING KIRTAN

What drew visitors to the Shahbagh Gardens was the divine bhav that Ma manifested during kirtan. At the sound of the holy name of God, Ma's body would undergo a miraculous transformation. As the devotees sang and danced to the accompaniment of *mridanga* and cymbals, Ma's body would become possessed by a divine power. Her countenance would be flushed crimson, and she would be lifted up on the very tips of her toes. Barely touching the floor, she would sway and flow through the crowd, to the rhythm of the music. Then, her body would drop to the ground, roll and float across the floor with the swiftness of lightning, only to be drawn up full-length, once again, with her arms over the head, swaying rhythmically with the cadence of the drums.

Those who witnessed these bhavas were overwhelmed by their beauty and grace, and felt the power and magnificence of God in her presence. At the end of the kirtan, Ma's body would sink to the floor in deep samadhi, and sacred mantras would issue from her mouth rapidly with perfect articulation. The radiance and majesty of her countenance while she was absorbed in a trance, moved everyone deeply.

One night, a violent rainstorm began during kirtan. Ma, in a divine bhav, led the kirtan party out into the rain and continued singing and dancing in the midst of the storm, taking on the very bhav of the storm itself. At this time, Ma's young niece, Labanya, was visiting Shahbagh. Seeing her aunt in this strange state, she ran up and hugged her. She was immediately flung backwards to the ground by the unrestrained power emanating from Ma during her bhav. In the darkness of the night, and the press of the crowd, the young girl was not noticed as she fell backwards on to the muddy ground.

When her family went looking for her, they saw what appeared to be a mound of earth, sweetly uttering the divine name Hari. They pulled the girl out of the mud, but found they could not restore her to normalcy. She had been lifted into a state of extreme spiritual exaltation by the power of Ma's touch during bhava. When told to stop repeating the name of Hari, she replied, *"I see the whole Universe as being filled with this name, so how can I stop saying it: Hari, Hari, Hari bol!"* Finally, her relatives brought her to Ma and asked that she be restored to her normal state of mind. Ma smilingly replied that yogis practice lifetimes of tapasya to attain such a state, yet they were asking her to take it from the child? But being pressed, she brought the girl back to her former state of consciousness.

TWO
MIRACLES

The miraculous and supernatural became the norm around Ma. Although she was not one to indulge in a pompous display of her powers, the line of distinction between what was 'normal' and 'supernormal' seemed to disappear in her presence. With Ma, everything came about naturally and spontaneously, and what was needed for the people's welfare was manifested of its own accord.

One day, a family brought their young daughter who was almost completely paralysed to Ma, who was peeling some betel nuts to be offered in the puja. Ma simply threw a few betel nuts on the floor, near the girl, and told her to pick them up. To the surprise of the parents, the girl, with great difficulty, was able to move and slowly pick them up. The family returned home and, later in the day, as the girl lay in bed, she heard a noisy, religious parade passing in the street below. Without thinking, she jumped up and ran to the window to witness the scene. It was only later that she realised she was completely cured!

A young couple, that had remained childless for years, came to ask if they could have children. As Ma came out of her room, the man approached and, kneeling, placed his head on her feet. At the touch, his consciousness was so transformed that he entered into a deep yogic trance, and remained absorbed in it for some time. He later returned home, so inwardly renewed that he completely forgot his request. Although he had not outwardly petitioned Ma, but had held it in his mind when he touched Ma's feet, his wife soon conceived and bore a lovely child.

Many people, while gazing on Ma, had visions of their own *ishta devta*. With open eyes, they would see Ma as Krishna or Kali, or in whatever form they held dear and divine.

NINE GRAINS
OF RICE

During these early days, Ma entered a state in which she no longer fed herself. She simply had no desire to eat or sustain her body. She told Didi, and those near her, that for her body to remain among them, it would be necessary for them to take care of it. From that day on, Ma was fed by hand like a child and never ate from her own hands. Her eating habits fell into a strange pattern. For months on end, she lived on exactly nine grains of rice a day. The grains would be carefully counted, and she would refuse anything beyond that. There would be long periods when she would eat nothing at all, followed by periods of eating small quantities of vegetables on alternate days, or perhaps only having some fruit or milk.

On one occasion, after her prolonged abstinence from food, the devotees got worried and beseeched her to take some food. Finally, at their insistence, Ma sat down to eat and, as Didi fed her, she continued to eat and eat! After consuming a huge quantity of food and showing no signs of stopping, the same devotees came with folded hands and begged her to stop eating. Ma laughed and said, *"You asked me to eat, and now you want me to stop. Please decide... to me it is all the same."* From then on, they learned not to interfere in Ma's behaviour.

Ma insisted that no provisions should be stored, but that food must be prepared from the ingredients at hand and distributed that same day. Bhaiji, out of concern for Ma's eating habits, once secretly bought a large supply of flour, *ghee* and vegetables, and gave it to Didi for Ma's use. That very morning when Ma arose, she asked Didi to prepare food using every available ingredient at hand. When the food was ready, Ma sat down to eat and went right on eating until she had consumed the entire, vast quantity of food all by herself. She then called Bhaiji and told him, *"Don't think of setting aside a stock of food for my use, nor be concerned about my not eating. If I did truly begin to eat, you people would never be able to provide for me!"*

There were several instances when Ma showed that the life of her body had no connection with the food she ate, or any other external factors. She often said that within all elements of nature there is an infinite supply of energy, and it is possible to be sustained even by light and air itself. She demonstrated this by going for long periods without any food at all, without exhibiting any diminution of energy or strength. Didi would also note, when dressing Ma, that on some days the same clothes would fit, and on other days they would be too small. Ma's size changed without any obvious reason. Even her height would change, sometimes appearing taller than at other times.

MA PERFORMS
NAMAAZ

Among the growing number of devotees who constantly surrounded Ma, were many Muslims who were also drawn to her presence. Within the grounds of the Shahbagh Gardens, was a tomb of a Muslim *fakir* and his disciple. One evening, as kirtan was going on in the hall, a Muslim man, who had heard of Ma, came and stood outside watching the festivities. His religious persuasion prevented him from entering a place where Hindu rituals were being performed. Suddenly, Ma came out of the hall and walking quickly by the man, motioned for him to follow. He, and several other Muslim devotees, followed Ma who led them to the tomb of the Muslim saint. Upon arriving, Ma spontaneously performed the complete service of the *Namaaz*, in faultless Arabic, with all the appropriate bows and gestures. As the man witnessed this, he was overcome and joined her in the devotions, pointing out afterwards how Ma had performed every little detail with perfect precision and beauty.

On another occasion, as Ma came out of the garden compound with Bhaiji and Didi, she hailed a passing taxi and the three climbed in. When asked by the young Muslim driver where they wanted to go, she replied, *"We will go to your house."* The young man complied and, upon arriving at his house, they found his father, who had been seriously ill, on the point of death. Ma had sweets brought, which she distributed to all and, blessing the man, returned to Shahbagh. Out of curiosity, Bhaiji returned to the driver's house the next day to find his father completely recovered, and the entire family in a state of great joy.

In 1929, a National Congress of Philosophers was held in Dhaka. Many of the participants in this gathering had heard the tales of the young Bengali Mataji and came to see her. They were told that she was virtually uneducated and very simple. The assembled group plied her with many complicated philosophical questions from the scriptures. To their amazement, Ma, sitting serenely and radiantly before them, answered every one of their queries without a moment's hesitation. The depth and profundity of her replies so impressed them, that in the end they folded their hands and told her, "We have studied dry scriptures. But, we now see before us, a living embodiment of all that is contained in our holy books of wisdom."

THE ADVENT OF
ANANDAMAYI MA

An ancient, abandoned Kali temple stood in the midst of the dense jungle around the Shahbagh Gardens. This temple had appeared many times in visions to Ma and one day, while walking in the forest, she came upon this temple which was hidden behind bushes. After this, Ma frequently visited this temple and stayed there, in the company of just one or two devotees. Bholanath would also come and spend time in solitary yogic practice. Once, in the early hours of the morning, Ma suddenly alerted Bholanath to follow her outdoors. She walked briskly, for a short distance away from the temple, and stopped in a small clearing. She then drew a circle on the ground, and reciting certain mantras, sat on the ground in the clearing, indicating that Bholanath should sit beside her. The earth was firm and dry underneath, but Ma suddenly started pushing her hand into the earth. Her arm slid deep into the ground, as if the earth was parting before her. When her arm was inserted all the way up to the shoulder, Bholanath became alarmed and forcefully withdrew Ma's arm from the ground. He found that she was holding an object in her hand that she had retrieved from deep below the ground. Upon having her arm withdrawn, warm, red-coloured water flowed from under the ground. Ma revealed that this site had been the place where yogis and saints had practiced their penance in a previous time, and Bholanath himself had lived there in a former life and performed tapasya there. The object in her hand had been something that Bholanath had used in his previous birth. The spot was marked and a platform was built where Ma would frequently sit.

As Ma began spending more time in the Siddheshwari Temple and sitting on this platform, devotees began to visit her there, also. One night, as a group of people was sitting with Ma, they witnessed an incredible yogic phenomenon. Several eyewitnesses saw to their amazement, Ma's form slowly shrink in size until nothing was left but a pile of empty clothes on the platform. Then, before their eyes, a movement started from within the empty bundle, and Ma's form slowly rose up again. Then, sitting motionless with her eyes turned upward, Ma spoke in a sweet, otherworldly voice explaining her real nature. She said, *"For your life's work, you have brought down this body. Your own aspiration has called it."*

One morning, Bhaiji was waiting outside Ma's room. Suddenly, the door flew open and revealed the radiant and flaming form of an ethereal goddess standing in the doorway. The light was slowly withdrawn into the body of the apparition, thereby revealing the form of Ma, who stood smiling at Bhaiji.

A rational man, Bhaiji hesitated to believe his own eyes, and thought: 'If what I have just seen is true, Ma will respond if I mentally recite mantras to the goddess.' So, he stood there mentally reciting verses in praise of the Divine Mother. Ma walked towards him, stopping briefly to pick some wild flowers along the path. As she drew near, he bowed before her, and she strewed the flowers over his head to acknowledge his unspoken prayer.

One day, at mid-morning, Ma called Bhaiji from his office. He came to the temple and found Ma sitting on the platform. As he sat in front of her and conversed, he observed that her countenance was so joyful and radiant, and her whole being radiated such bliss that he told Bholanath, "From this moment we will call Ma, 'Anandamayi Ma' (Bliss Permeated Mother)." Bholanath agreed wholeheartedly. When Bhaiji later asked Ma why she had called him, she laughingly replied, *"How else would I have gotten my name today?"* From then onward, devotees have addressed Ma by this name and received her response.

Now Ma, along with a small *toli* of devotees, made a trip to the ancient city of Varanasi (formerly known as Benares). News of her arrival spread through word-of-mouth, and the place where she was staying became a scene of uninterrupted festivity, with a stream of visitors coming and going all through the day and night. Bholanath at first objected, but Ma reminded him that he had earlier given his permission for people to approach her whenever they wished. *"Now it will be impossible to close the gates that you have opened,"* she told him. He accepted this willingly, and soon found his own place as the loving father and guide of the growing family of devotees that surrounded Ma.

One of the visitors who came to Ma was Gopinath Kaviraj, a renowned scholar and saintly person. He was recognised as one of India's greatest contemporary *pandits*. Kaviraj saw in Ma, the states and manifestations that he had only read of in the shastras. Highly impressed, he stayed near Ma whenever it was possible for him to do so, and eventually spent the last years of his life in Ma's ashram in Varanasi.

Returning to Bengal, Bholanath spent a long time at the ancient holy site of Tarapeeth engaged in intense yogic practice and meditation, reaching very exalted states of consciousness. Ma came and stayed with him for long periods and became popular among the local people. The women of Tarapeeth told Ma that they recognised her as the Devi Herself. In Ma's presence, Bholanath began to impart diksha to those who petitioned him. Over the next few years, several people received initiation from him and looked upon him as their guru.

Thanks to Bhaiji's effort, a small ashram was eventually established in 1932 at Ramna, on the outskirts of Dhaka, and a smaller hermitage built next to the Siddheshwari Temple. These were to be the first of many ashrams built in Ma's name. They became places of intense joy and activity, centered around Ma's radiant presence. Kirtans, festivals, and spiritual practices were always being conducted, with Ma giving instruction and guidance to everyone who came to the ashrams.

Anandamayi in a state of Mahabhav

A FAREWELL
TO BENGAL

After being in the midst of devotees in Dhaka for eight years, Ma suddenly left Bengal in 1932. The day prior to her departure, while everyone was still blissfully ignorant of it, Ma set out from the ashram early in the morning, with the words, *"Come, let us go and collect bhiksha."* People from the ashram followed and the joyful sport of Ma continued all day. She went to every devotee's house, and standing outside, begged for bhiksha. The residents happily joined in the game, giving provisions from their house, and then joining the band of people as they moved to the next house. At the end of the day, all the devotees were following Ma as she walked through the town, while the provisions they had collected filled a whole rickshaw that trailed them.

Returning to the ashram, Ma gave instructions that a feast should be prepared with the provisions they had collected. Everyone joined in the preparations, Ma herself lending a hand in cooking and serving the food. Late at night, all the devotees left the ashram filled with great joy and contentment, not knowing that this had been Ma's farewell to them. With only the few ashram dwellers remaining, Ma called them one by one and spoke with each of them privately, revealing that she was leaving that very night for an unknown destination. Amidst the protests, she requested, *"Allow me to move about according to my kheyal. I cannot if you put obstacles in my path."*

She called Bholanath to seek his permission and seeing she was determined to go, Bholanath assented and awaited her instructions. Ma asked for Bhaiji to be called from his home. On being told that he would be accompanying Ma, he asked to return home so he could inform his family. Ma denied his request and, collecting funds from the people present, set off for the railway station with Bholanath and Bhaiji. When asked what their destination would be, she instructed that they should buy tickets to wherever the railway line terminated. Ma left Bengal in the middle of the night, without funds or luggage, or even a set destination, guided only by her kheyal. When the devotees of Dhaka spoke among themselves about these strange events, they found that in the days preceding her departure, Ma had spoken privately to every single person without the others knowing it, giving detailed instructions and encouragement for their spiritual practice. Thus began the odyssey that would continue for the remaining fifty years of Ma's life. From this point onward, Ma ceaselessly wandered throughout India, never remaining in one place for a long time.

Anandamayi among her devotees

SOJOURN IN
THE HIMALAYAS

Travelling without any planned itinerary, the three pilgrims eventually reached the small town of Dehradun, at the foothills of the Himalayas. Here, they settled in a small, abandoned building adjoining an ancient Shiva temple near the small village of Raipur, and spent six months living simply and in seclusion. Bholanath continued his intensive spiritual practice, spending most of his days in meditation. Most of the time, Ma would just be sitting or lying in a state of samadhi, or walking idly through the nearby fields and forests. Bhaiji, who always had servants and employees to do his slightest bidding, joyfully applied himself to menial labour to care for the needs of the two people he regarded as the father and mother of his soul. He went out to collect bhiksha from the nearby village, cooked the meals and washed the clothes, living like a simple sadhu.

Eventually, the news filtered out that a strange Bengali

Mataji was staying in the old temple, and people began coming in the evening to see her. Drawn first by simple curiosity, they were at once impressed by Ma's personality and began to return regularly, the group of visitors increasing daily. Ma never delivered formal lectures, but would sit informally and answer any questions that were asked. Ma, earlier speaking only in Bengali, now started speaking in Hindi spontaneously, after a few weeks. Her face would flush and with her eyes overflowing with bliss and love, divine wisdom would pour from her mouth, elucidating every aspect of spiritual life. All those who saw her felt she was their very own, dearer than their closest relative. Ma would always say of those that came to her, *"No one is new to me. All are always familiar."* To those people who had braved the treacherous path to the deserted temple to spend hours sitting at her feet, she would say, *"Whether you know it or not, I am your nearest and dearest – your very own Self."* A new circle of devotees grew rapidly in this deserted place.

One prominent devotee was Hari Ram Joshi from Dehradun, who occupied a prominent place in society. He became a life-long devotee, bringing many important people to Ma, including some famous political leaders of the time. Kamala Nehru, Jawaharlal Nehru, and eventually Indira Gandhi became devotees of Ma. Hari Ram also played a large part in founding the first ashram at Dehradun.

After six months in Raipur, Bholanath left to visit the northern Himalayan shrines, settling in Uttarkashi to pass several years in asceticism and meditation. Ma and Bhaiji wandered alone, and occasionally in the company of other devotees, through many of the towns and villages, living as simple sadhus. They slept on the verandahs of temples or in rest houses made for pilgrims, led by Ma's spontaneous kheyal.

In 1933, Bholanath sent word that with the help of some friends, he was establishing a small Kali temple at the place where he was practicing meditation in Uttarkashi. For the opening of the temple, Ma sent word to Gurupriya Didi and her father, who were in Bengal, to come along with any of the devotees who wished to accompany them. Her new band of devotees in and around Dehradun opened their hearts and homes for the devotees who arrived from Bengal. When everyone had assembled, they walked with Ma along the mountainous trail from Mussoorie to Uttarkashi to join Bholanath in the inauguration of the Kali temple. The trek took several days and was fraught with difficulties, but everyone felt joyous and uplifted in Ma's presence. At one point, having to cross a rapidly flowing stream, Ma stood in the middle and helped each pilgrim across. The powerful image of Ma standing in the middle of the torrents, firmly assisting each devotee's crossing, so impressed the minds of onlookers that they prayed to Ma with joined hands, "Ma, also assist us across the *bhava nadi* in this same manner!"

From now onward, Didi and her father would continue to stay with Ma. Didi took formal monastic vows of *Brahmacharya*. Didi's father, who was the head of a large clan of Bengalis and a prominent member of society, was slowly weaned from his worldly pursuits and lifestyle by Ma, who began instructing him in spiritual practices and moulding him into an exemplary ascetic. He eventually left everything and took the formal vow of *sanyas*, becoming Ma's first monastic follower with the new name of Swami Akhandananda Giri.

At one point in Ma's wanderings in the foothills of the Himalayas, she was staying in a small cave, near the hill station of Shimla, with just Bhaiji and one other devotee. It was here that Raja Durga Singh, a local Raja who was the ruler of Solan, heard of her. A man of sterling character and religious disposition, he was always seeking the company of saints and religious leaders. He came to visit Ma, and found her sitting at total ease in the intense cold and dampness of the rugged hillside cave. Upon seeing her blissful countenance and hearing her inspired words, the Raja became an ardent devotee, frequently inviting Ma and her entire entourage to stay on the grounds of his palace. Ma gave him the name Yogibhai because of his intense practice of yoga and meditation. Raja Durga Singh's family, and later his court, became Ma's devotees.

Ma always stressed that spiritual attainment can be achieved by a sincere and sustained repetition of the name of God. She said, *"Always bear in mind that God's name is He Himself. Let it be your inseparable companion. Since all names are His indeed, He will allow Himself to be grasped by any one of them."* This was illustrated in her own life. The most dramatic illustration was the divine bhav that manifested during kirtan, at different periods in her life. In the years following her departure from Shahbagh Gardens, there were no manifestations of this kind for an extended period. But, once again in 1936, the devotees were privileged to witness this awesome manifestation.

While in Shimla, Ma was invited to attend the annual celebrations of a local religious sect. As part of the festivities, everyone spent an unbroken twelve hours walking slowly around a beautifully decorated altar, placed in the middle of a large hall, while melodiously chanting the holy names of God to the accompaniment of drums and cymbals. At the very commencement of the chanting, a palpable spiritual atmosphere was created. Bholanath and Didi noticed that Ma was overcome and was beginning to enter a deep inner state. Bholanath requested Ma to control herself, as he was not sure how strangers would respond to Ma's spontaneous manifestations. Didi noticed Ma's efforts to contain the spiritual current that was rising within her, as it was reflected in her face and movements.

At different points in the course of the day, a bright light would play across Ma's countenance, or her gaze would become fixed as she would be transported into a yogic samadhi. In the concluding ceremony, Ma suddenly stood up and walked into the midst of the crowd of singers. Her movements were as swift as lightning. At times she could only be seen as a blur of white as the tide of Mahabhav animated her body. The participants in the kirtan witnessed what they had only read of in their scriptures. At the end of the kirtan, Ma sank to the floor and, while she was in this deeply absorbed state, holy mantras emanated from her mouth in a sweet and enchanting voice. The people knelt around her in reverence, reciting hymns to the Devi. They made Ma promise that she would attend the celebration every year, and from then onward, her picture adorned the hall where the festival took place.

Wherever Ma went, she encouraged the women to also participate in the kirtan. In those days, only men sang during kirtan while the women listened from a separate room. Ma suggested that the women also should join in the singing during the festivities. She asked the men not to leave their wives out of this important spiritual practice. Soon, women began to gather for their own kirtan session, Ma walking and singing with them, and encouraging them in their efforts.

Anandamayi Ma with Indira Gandhi and Jawaharlal Nehru

IN THE ABODE
OF SHIVA

I n 1937, Ma was visiting Mussoorie, a small hill resort about
22 kms. from Dehradun. Here, she met some young girls
who were studying in college. These girls were from a village
north of Almora, and lived a short distance from the holy
mountain of Kailash, which is considered the most important,
although one of the most difficult to reach pilgrimage shrines
in India. Traditionally considered to be the abode of Lord Shiva,
it is situated high amidst the rugged wilderness of the
Himalayan ranges.

The students invited Ma to join them on their return
home, promising that they would guide and accompany her
to Kailash. Bholanath had an adventurous spirit and was
fond of pilgrimages. He was enthusiastic at the proposal.
So, Ma and a small group made arrangements for the difficult
journey. Accompanying Ma would be Bholanath, Didi,
Swami Akhandananda and Bhaiji, in addition to the two

girls from Mussoorie. After arranging for the necessary warm clothing, horses and supplies, the party started from Almora, on a pass that cuts through the mountain ranges. Bad weather, the threat of dacoits, and virtually impassable terrain made the journey quite difficult. However, the party proceeded happily in Ma's company, spurred on by the awesome grandeur of the mountainous landscape.

Even the simple hill people were attracted to Ma's mystic aura. One day, when the travellers were resting by the side of the trail, a village woman passed carrying a bundle of wood on her head. Ma greeted her in her friendly manner and the lady smiled and continued on her way. Didi, who witnessed this exchange, recounted how she saw the woman stop and, turning back, looked long at Ma, then returned to sit by her with an awed expression and speak, opening her heart in love. The villagers who met Ma began addressing her as *Devi Bhagavati*.

One day, as the pilgrims entered a narrow pass in the high mountains, they were confronted by a band of heavily-armed bandits at the end of the gorge. The local guide who was leading the pilgrims, spurred his horse and galloped ahead to meet the leader of the bandits. He told him that Ma and her followers were on a pilgrimage to Mount Kailash. As the dacoit gazed on Ma's face, something from within prompted him to simply let them pass, and Ma alongwith her party rode past the bandits without being harmed in any way.

Upon reaching Lake Mansarovar, close to Mount Kailash,

Bhaiji was gripped by an intense feeling of renunciation, and requested Ma's permission to spend the remainder of his life in one of the nearby caves, practicing meditation. In response to his deep yearning, the holy mantras for sanyas spontaneously issued from Ma's mouth. She asked him to remain with them, but gave him the monastic name of Swami Maunananda Parvat.

During the day, spent along the vast, beautiful lake, the sight of the holy mountain of Kailash towering in the distance, and the air of holiness surrounding the place, affected everyone very deeply. Bholanath was walking with Ma and, in accordance with his inner desire, he received the sanyas mantra which spontaneously issued from Ma's lips. He later confirmed these vows formally in Haridwar.

After completing the circumambulation of the holy mountain, they returned to Almora. Along the way, Bhaiji became very ill and, upon arriving in Almora, was in a critical condition. Doctors were consulted, and Ma lovingly nursed him, rarely leaving his bedside. In his dying moments, he repeated the sanyas mantra and, with his eyes fixed on Ma, repeated her name several times and closed his eyes in peace.

THE KUMBH MELA
OF HARIDWAR

In 1938, Ma and her devotees attended the great religious gathering of *Kumbh Mela* at Haridwar. Every day, Bholanath would take a large group of kirtan singers into the city, chanting the holy name of God in the streets. His striking appearance and the fervour of his devotion always attracted a crowd, and many pilgrims would join the group and take up the refrain of the chant.

During the Kumbh Mela, there are certain astrological periods when bathing in the holy Ganga river is considered very auspicious. On one such day, Bholanath went down to bathe in the Ganga. To his surprise, the large gathering of sadhus assembled there received him with great reverence, and ritually bathed him with their own hands. When Ma was told of this, she commented, *"Bholanath lives in self-forgetfulness, but the sadhus recognised his spiritual greatness."* At this time, Bholanath made took the formal vows of sanyas.

Shortly after leaving Haridwar, Bholanath contracted smallpox and was taken to recuperate at the Dehradun ashram. For fear of infection, Ma ordered most of the inmates away, and personally nursed Bholanath till the very end. After seeking Ma's forgiveness for any mistake he may have inadvertently committed in her service, he addressed her as "Ma" and, while she held her hand on the top of his head, he passed away, under her protection. Later, when asked why she didn't seem to grieve over the loss of her husband, she replied, *"How can I grieve? I can see clearly where the soul is and where it has gone!"*

In 1939, Ma's mother, Mokshada Sundari, took the vows of renunciation, assuming the name Swami Muktananda Giri. Now Ma addressed her as Giriji. To the devotees, she was still known as Didima. A woman of remarkable and saintly character, Didima began to play an increasingly important role in the life of Ma. She had reached a high level of spirituality, having spent many years in ascetic discipline and meditation. She began travelling with Ma. After Bholanath's passing, Didima began imparting initiation to people in Ma's presence, and giving spiritual direction as a guru.

THE WANDERING
PILGRIMS

Ma continued on her travels prompted by the heartfelt call of her devotees. For several months, she travelled completely incognito with just one companion, a woman ascetic named Biraj Mohini Didi. Travelling without money or baggage, the two led the life of wandering pilgrims; blessing everyone they met with their joyful and uplifting presence. At other times, Ma would be surrounded by throngs of devotees, who stayed with her day and night, receiving her guidance, and expressing their love and devotion in different ways. There would be days, when Ma would remain sitting in one place for fourteen or fifteen hours at a stretch, greeting the influx of visitors with the same blissful and loving smile, showing no signs of fatigue. Close devotees, who tried unsuccessfully to manage the influx of people and allow Ma to rest for some time, asked her if the constant push of the crowd bothered her. She replied, *"Are you annoyed if your own hand touches your leg or another part of your body? To me, there is only the One, and all are His manifestations. You and I are one, and the space between us is also myself."*

There are innumerable incidents of Ma being drawn to a particular place by the sincere call from a devotee's heart. One old and infirm sadhu, in the coastal city of Puri, had been longing for Ma's *darshan*, but because of his age and infirmity was unable to make the journey, and so only prayed to her in his heart. Ma, who was far away at the time, suddenly changed her plans and made an unexpected trip to Puri. One day, to the sadhu's surprise, she simply walked into his room and sat next to his bed and spoke with him for a long time.

Another time, Ma was seated at a religious function, when she suddenly got up and left the gathering, followed by Didi and one or two other devotees. She went directly to the railway station and boarded a waiting train. Getting down at a small station where the train usually did not stop, and followed by her bewildered companions, she walked briskly through the town to a small rest house for pilgrims. She went directly towards one room without asking directions and entered inside. There was a woman sitting on the bed, and weeping inconsolably. Ma simply said, *"Don't weep. See, I have come."* The surprised woman's tears turned to ones of joy and gratitude. Upon composing herself, she told Didi that she had come to this small town on receiving information that Ma would be there, but on finding that Ma was somewhere far away, had retired to the lonely room where she tearfully poured forth her grief and longing for Ma. Time and space were non-existent for Ma, and she always responded to the true longing of the heart. Ma has said, *"Your sorrow, your pain, your agony is indeed my sorrow. This body understands everything."* (Ma would frequently refer to herself as 'this body', having no feeling of herself as a separate entity from God.)

Anandamayi Ma greets her devotees at a religious function

MA MEETS
MAHATMA GANDHI

During the restless 1940s that witnessed India's struggle for independence, many freedom fighters came to meet Ma to seek her blessings. Ma's consciousness never descended to the level of politics, but she did encourage the people by saying that since God had inspired them with this ideal, He would work His will through them. In 1941, Seth Jamnalal Bajaj, a close co-worker of Mahatma Gandhi, came to visit Ma. He was planning to stay only a short time, but was so captivated by Ma that he wired Gandhiji for permission to stay longer. He surrendered himself to Ma and found such peace in her presence that he did not want to leave. After some time, she sent him back to Wardha to continue his work, giving him instructions for continuing his spiritual life, and a greeting for the Mahatma.

Through the sincere efforts of both Kamala Nehru and Sethji, a meeting was arranged between Ma and Mahatma

Gandhi. Upon entering his room, Ma cried out, *"Father! Your crazy daughter has come to visit you!"* Gandhiji received her with open arms and sat holding her hand and together they conversed happily for a long time. He requested her to stay with him longer, but Ma only responded with laughter and quick-witted humour. At one point during the conversation, Ma spoke gravely to Gandhiji and told him, *"I shall come and take you at the appropriate time."* Upon leaving, he scolded Ma and said, "You have come like a dacoit to steal my heart!" Ma laughingly replied, *"I shall steal everything belonging to you; shall I?"* To which the Mahatma replied softly, "Such theft is a rare fortune." Later, to one of his assistants, she sent the message, *"Tell Mahatmaji to be prepared. After all, the time for going home is drawing near."*

Ma met Gandhiji once again, shortly before his assassination in 1948. He again asked her to stop wandering and stay with him. She blessed him saying, *"Father believe me, I am always with you."* At one time or another, all the newly elected leaders of the Indian Republic came for her darshan and blessings.

IN THE COMPANY
OF SADHUS

Up till now, only a few members of the established monastic orders had come to visit Ma. These sanyasis, being of a very orthodox outlook, generally viewed Ma as a simple Bengali widow, with no guru or *sampradaya*. A great saint by the name of Sri Prabhudatta Brahmachari had a high regard for Ma, and wanted to introduce her to the community of sadhus that led and set the standards for the Hindu community. In 1944, at his ashram in Jhansi, Prabhudatta organised a huge gathering of sadhus and religious leaders, and invited Ma as one of the main guests. After a week in this gathering, everyone recognised in Ma the embodiment of the high ideal for which they were striving. Many widely acclaimed saints became Ma's intimate devotees. Among them were the beloved Haribaba of Baandh, Uriyababa and Swami Akhandananda of Vrindavan. From now on, many saints and sanyasis graced the functions of Ma's ashrams with their presence. Ma was also invited and given a place of honour by the great gathering of sadhus at the various Kumbh Melas.

Anandamayi Ma with Bholanath (left) and Swami Paramhansa Yogananda

THE SAVITRI
MAHAYAJNA

Political and cultural unrest was brewing in 1947. Ma felt that a great *yajna* should be organised to facilitate the release of vast amounts of energy and divine blessings on a needy world. This finally culminated in the *Savitri Mahayajna*, which was performed at the Varanasi ashram. A yajna is a *Vedic* ritual in which blessings and power are invoked through mantras and offerings that are poured into a sacred fire, with strict adherence to the guidelines laid down in the scriptures.

The powerful *Gayatri Mantra* was chosen to be recited during the yajna, and the intention was to seek the well-being of all humankind. The rituals began on a modest scale, and it seemed that all the necessary elements for the ritual, including the volunteers needed for the yajna, came of their own accord. Ma took great interest in the ceremonies and was often in Varanasi during the next three years, directing and supervising the proceedings. As the months passed, the yajna grew in size and strength. The ashram now resembled a small city of workers, preparing offerings, decorating the ashram, and doing every service that was required for the smooth performance of the powerful yajna.

On 14th January, 1950, the *purnahuti* took place. Thousands of devotees from all over the country were in attendance, and many famous saints and *mahatmas* graced the function. Many feel that the great power released through the performance of this ancient ritual during these years was one of the stabilising forces for the days before and following Indian Independence, in addition to helping the whole world, during the difficult years following the Second World War.

IN THE PRESENCE
OF GRACE

What did people experience in Ma's presence that made them seek her company again and again? In her, they felt many of their deepest needs and longings being recognised and addressed. If a hundred people were sitting in front of her, if they were inwardly attuned to her, each one felt that he or she was receiving Ma's complete attention and love. Awakening of the mind and awareness of the consciousness spontaneously arose in people who were simply sitting in front of Ma. They were filled with happiness and bliss from within. A festive atmosphere prevailed with the singing of kirtan and the recitation of the holy scriptures.

At times, Ma would walk into a village and the devotees with her would start singing kirtan. As the group advanced, many would come and join in, and by the time they reached the temple or shrine that they were visiting, a festive air would encompass the entire village. At Navadweep in Bengal, Ma was walking with her followers when, suddenly, she headed toward the local police station. The Superintendent of Police came out and welcomed her with great joy. He confessed that he had been longing to see her, but hadn't been able to get away from his duties. Some of the village folk passing by the gates of the station saw Ma seated in the compound surrounded by her devotees, and called out, "Ma, have they arrested you?" The Superintendent, to everyone's amusement loudly responded, "Yes! I've arrested her for stealing my mind and heart!"

On being asked why she continually roamed from one place to another, Ma would say that only we saw her moving. She felt as if she were only moving from one room of her house to another, and, therefore, not really moving at all.

Ma's departure from a place even after a short stay, would leave most people weeping as Ma's train pulled out of the station. But through this very process, what a valuable lesson Ma taught those came into contact with her: The cause of man's ignorance and suffering is his complacency towards God and things spiritual, and his selfish obsession with the things of this world. Reading in the scriptures that we should redirect our minds from our own small world to God can have little effect, if not experienced directly and personally. Many who met Ma had no previous interest in spirituality. All they knew was that Ma evoked a powerful and profound effect over them, and they longed to be in her presence. Her very presence inspired love for God in everyone. Ma has said, *"The search after Truth is the one thing by which the shape of human life should be determined. Genuine desire itself opens the road to fulfillment.*" By her departure, which left them grieving, the very longing and restlessness for God, which is itself the path to God, was kindled and awakened. People were shaken and disturbed from their complacent sleep of worldliness, not by eloquent sermons and scriptural quotes, but by Ma's personal, loving presence to which people responded from their hearts.

TEACHING BY
EXAMPLE

I n 1952, following a suggestion from Ma, the first *Samyam Saptah* was organised. Ma said that everyone should try to privately observe at regular intervals, what they considered to be a perfect day of spirituality. On this day, all observances such as taking only moderate quantities of pure food, talking less or observing silence, spending time in meditation and contemplation, should be scrupulously followed. She said that if this was observed regularly, worldly tendencies and habits could be weakened, and such a way of life would become the natural observance, greatly strengthening one's spiritual life. The devotees approached Ma with the idea of having a week of such observance followed by the entire gathering. Ma readily agreed and from this time onwards took a great and active interest in this yearly observance, personally outlining many points in the daily schedule. Many mahatmas were invited to give talks on spiritual life. People attended the gathering from all walks of life, many of whom lived very luxurious and indulgent lives. All were wondering if this week would be possible for them, being so accustomed to comfort and ease in their normal daily lives. The participants found that not only was the week's programme possible for them, but that in Ma's presence and in following such a strict regimen they found great joy and benefit. They found that following the formal week of restraint, they were able to introduce more spiritual and ascetic practices into their own daily schedules. The Samyam Saptah became an annual, well-attended function and continues in Ma's ashrams to this day.

Ma spoke of no 'new' way, nor did she have a special message. Her whole emphasis was on following the time-honoured path of tradition. She advocated belief in the scriptures and the rituals of religious ceremonies. The way she lived her life, paved the way for a renewed role for women both in spiritual life and society in general. Women had free access to Ma and were able to live in close proximity to her and render personal service. At every stage of her life, she showed how each stage of life should be perfectly lived, so it becomes a clear and easy path to God.

Everywhere Ma went, she advocated women taking a turn in singing at public kirtans, and encouraged men to include their wives in all their spiritual strivings. Ma revived the ancient practice of the sacred thread ceremony, and gave the benediction of the Gayatri Mantra to girls as well as boys. Some women in her entourage were instructed by her in wearing of the sacred thread. The girls in the Kanyapeeth – the girl's school at the Varanasi ashram, under Ma's supervision and guidance, excelled in their studies and went on to either embrace a life of renunciation and spiritual endeavour, or entered their domestic lives fully trained and confident in their abilities. Ma always stressed the importance of women's role in society, and the need for mutual respect between the sexes.

Devotees from all walks of life found great joy and benefit in Ma's presence

THE HELPING HAND
OF MA

Many stories are told of Ma's ever-present hand of protection over her devotees. One evening, a family arrived late for Ma's *satsang* and, upon entering the hall, asked Ma's permission to tell everyone what had befallen them on their way to the ashram. As they were coming in their car, the person behind the wheel had lost control along the winding, mountainous road. On a sharp turn, the car suddenly seemed to be headed off a cliff over a deep chasm. Everyone spontaneously cried out "MA!" At once they saw Ma's form appear in the air underneath the car, and firmly and powerfully thrust the vehicle away from the cliff and back on to the road where it came to a halt.

One man told of his experience during the days of political unrest. He had been captured by a group of ruffians and tied to a chair in their hideout. In his presence, they discussed how they would murder him and dispose of his body. As they came forward to kill him, he prayed to Ma. His captors suddenly froze with fear for no apparent reason, and then quickly unbound him and sent him on his way unharmed.

A devotee, while bathing in the Ganga, was swept away by the current. At that exact moment, hundreds of miles away, Ma was sitting inside her room at one of the ashrams. Suddenly, her clothes became soaked with water, as if she had just had a bath. Didi immediately changed her clothes, but recorded the exact time of this incident, to see if she could unravel the mystery later. When the devotee recounted the day and the time that he was miraculously saved from the river, Didi discovered that it was the exact time that Ma's clothes had become mysteriously drenched.

Yet another devotee, Swami Virajananda, had a close encounter and narrow escape from a tiger while walking along a deserted mountain path. Sometime later, he was walking with Ma along the very same path, and at the place of the incident, Ma suddenly asked him, *"This is the very place that you were nearly attacked by the tiger, isn't it?"* The Swami was amazed and asked Ma how she could possibly know of this event, as he had never told anyone. Ma simply replied, *"Don't you know that this body is always near all of you?"*

One evening during satsang, Ma suddenly called several attendants and told them to immediately bring splints, bandages, hot water, and different materials for administering first aid. When all these items were assembled and brought to her, the satsang went on as before. Suddenly, a devotee who had been seriously injured in an accident while on his way to the ashram, was brought in. He was treated and bandaged under Ma's supervision and a doctor was sent for. When the doctor arrived, he looked at the patient and declared that everything had been perfectly accomplished, and there was nothing more for him to do.

A devotee in England recalled how one night he had decided to write a letter to Ma concerning a particular problem he was facing. In his mind he formulated the letter, intending to write it the next morning. To his surprise, he found that in his morning post there was a letter that Ma had dictated and sent to him some weeks ago! It contained a precise answer to the problem that he had posed in his mind only the night before!

On one occasion, a family was returning home after visiting Ma. On the way back, they had an accident and their car started to slide into a river. One of the girls quickly grasped a garland of flowers that had been given to her by Ma and said, "We have Ma's garland, so nothing can happen to us." They were saved from the brink of disaster and continued on their journey, and in the course of time even forgot about the accident. After six long years, this family again came to visit Ma. When they came near Ma and began to pay their respects, Ma looked at the girl and said, *"Ah... you are the one who said, 'We have Ma's garland, so nothing can happen to us!'"*

Ma's kindness and compassion knew no limits. A young man,

residing in one of the ashrams, was presenting such a problem by his behaviour that the inmates of the ashram had to bring the matter to Ma's attention. She called the boy and everyone in the ashram together to discuss the matter. After hearing the complaints, and the unanimous insistence that he should be expelled from the ashram, Ma turned her compassionate glance upon him and declared, *"Since all of you are against this poor wayward boy, then how can I also be? He needs me more than ever."* So saying, she patted his head as he burst into tears. Witnessing Ma's mercy, the inmates had a change of attitude towards the boy, and he, responding to her love, rectified his behaviour and became an ideal devotee.

Another time, during a satsang, a deranged-looking man in dishevelled clothes came to Ma. He started rebuking the women present there for not covering their heads. In response, Ma covered her own head, and all the women followed her example. This still did not pacify the man, and he continued being a nuisance. Ma gave him an orange, which for some reason seemed to enrage him, and he threw it back, hitting her squarely. This infuriated everyone, and some men from the audience hustled him out of the door. He tried to turn and come back towards Ma, but one of the men struck him and threw him outside. When the men returned, Ma rebuked their well-meaning attempts at order, saying that no one should be prevented from coming to her. The next day, to everyone's surprise, the same man came again to the satsang. His appearance had greatly changed. He was neatly dressed, looked calm, and sat quietly. He later told Ma that he had been suffering from a mental illness for many years. The previous day, he had felt such remorse for throwing the orange at Ma that he thought of her for the rest of the day, and that remembrance alone had completely cured his mental malady.

There are several instances of Ma being present by the deathbed of her devotees, assuring that they have a peaceful passing. Once, an elderly, sick lady was brought to the satsang hall at the Varanasi ashram. Ma had her laid on the floor at the back of the hall, and all through the evening's activities, she would periodically call out to her, *"Mataji, are you saying your japa?"* Suddenly, towards the end of the evening, Ma quickly rose to her feet and walked to the back of the hall. Looking at the woman with great compassion, she sprinkled *gangajal* over her and placed a garland on her chest. Then she ran her hands over the woman's form, from head to toe, and the lady breathed her last.

At the small ashram in the village of Naimashrayanya, there was a beloved disciple of Ma, known as Indu Ma. She had reached an advanced age and had fallen ill. In the night, she took a turn for the worse and it was decided to take her to the city hospital for treatment. While arrangements were being made for her transportation, Ma suddenly came out of her room, and walking quickly while saying, *"Indu Ma!"* she sat in front of the ashram temple. Shortly after, people came carrying Indu Ma in a chair towards the waiting car. They stopped in front of Ma, and Indu Ma raised her eyes to Ma's face, lifted her hands in *pranam*, and left her body peacefully.

THE CALL OF
THE UNMANIFEST

Almost thirty years after the Savitri Mahayajna, another great yajna was held under Ma's supervision. This was the *Atirudra Yajna*, performed at Ma's ashram in Kankhal, a small village near Haridwar. All the arrangements for this great yajna were made by Ma's *brahmacharinis*. All the scriptural injunctions were observed, and a new hall was built especially for the performance of the rituals. The intention was the general upliftment of all humankind. During the eleven days of the rituals, thousands of people came to walk the narrow path around the building as the priests chanted Vedic mantras around eleven sacrificial fires. The *Shankaracharya* of Sringeri made a special appearance at this yajna.

For some time prior to this yajna, Ma's health had been poor and she was seen to withdraw more into herself. Though she was constantly travelling, she was less active in public functions. After the yajna in Kankhal, the Shankaracharya asked Ma to turn her kheyal towards rejuvenating her body and health so that she would stay longer with her devotees. Ma answered, *"Father, what you see is not ill health. It is the call of the Unmanifest, and all that is happening is simply a response to this call."*

Then, Ma went back to her ashram at Kishenpur in Dehradun. It was here that Bholanath had left his mortal body over forty years ago. Ma's eating habits had always been sparse, but now she grew weaker by the day. Several doctors came to see her but they could not diagnose any specific illness. Ma was simply not showing any interest in her health. When asked why she was being so negligent, she replied, *"There is no illness here; only the friction between the manifest and the Unmanifest."*

Ma had now completely stopped eating any kind of food and would occasionally take just a few sips of water. A life-long devotee tried to persuade her to take some interest in her health by declaring, "Ma! I will not return home until I see you sitting up." Ma simply smiled, but later that day asked her attendants to prop her up in the bed. When this devotee came to take his leave, he found Ma sitting upright and looking at him with a calm and deep look of infinite compassion. In that moment, he inwardly realised that rather than this being a symptom of recovery, it was Ma's continued mercy for fulfilling her devotees' wishes.

Despite everyone's intense desire for Ma's recovery, certain signs of her approaching end began to get noticed. At one point, Ma uttered the mantra of Shiva in reverse:

"Shivaya namah!" In the Shaivaite scriptures, this reversal of the mantra is an invocation of dissolution and the breaking of all bonds. A devotee asked her to give a message for all her devotees. The final utterance of Ma was: *"Wherever you are, immerse yourself totally in one-pointed sadhana."*

On 27th August, 1982, Ma left her body, at her ashram in Dehradun. She was eighty-six years old at the time. Members of the ancient monastic orders took immediate charge, and a motorcade carrying her body was organised from Dehradun to Haridwar. The entire length of the road was lined with people paying their respects to the last darshan of Ma. Prime Minister Indira Gandhi, a life-long devotee of Ma, came to officiate at the last rites. Ma's body was placed in a sitting position in a specially built marble mausoleum, in the ashram at Kankhal. To this day, the beautiful *Jyoti Peeth* where her body is enshrined, radiates peace and blessings to the whole world.

Ever since Ma's passing from this world, devotees continue to have experiences of her unfailing protection and guidance. Her presence has been felt and seen many times by devotees in visions and dreams. Many people who weren't able to meet Ma in her physical body, still feel the warmth and attraction of her magical presence when they turn to her in prayer. The transcriptions of Ma's words and teachings are eternally relevant and enlivening. Ma has told us, *"It cannot be that anybody, anywhere is not my very own. I am with you at all times."*

Anandamayi Ma showering prasad on her devotees at a satsang

WORDS OF WISDOM
FROM MA

Ma said: *"This body tells of one sovereign remedy for all ills: God. Trust in Him, depend on Him, accept whatever happens as His dispensation, regard what you do as His service, keep satsang, think of God with every breath, and live in His presence. Leave all your burdens in His hands and He will see to everything; there will be no more problems.*

"All this, which is His creation, is under His dispensation, in His Presence, and is verily He Himself. In whatever state He keeps anyone at any time, it is all for the good, for verily everything is ordained by Him, and is of Him. Relative happiness, which is happiness depending on anything, must end in grief. It is man's duty to meditate on God who is peace Itself. Without having recourse to that which aids the remembrance of God, there can be no peace. Have you not seen what life in this world is? The One to be loved is God. In Him is everything — Him you must try to find.

"To a human being, the most noble, irreproachable line of conduct should alone be acceptable. It is a matter of great rejoicing if anyone strives to mould his life upon this pattern. Only actions that kindle man's divine nature are worthy of the name of action, all the rest are non-actions — a waste of energy. Any line of behaviour that fails to quicken the divine in man should be eschewed, no matter how enticing it might appear; but any that helps to awaken man's inherent divinity must be resolutely adopted, even though it be seemingly uninviting. Man's calling is to aspire to the realisation of Truth, to tread the excellent path that leads to immortality. What appears delightful to the senses later develops into a hotbed of poison, generating inner turmoil and disaster, for it belongs to the realm of death.

"In whichever direction you may turn your gaze, you will find One Eternal Indivisible Being manifested. Yet it is not at all easy to detect this presence, because He interpenetrates everything. As a king is known by his majesty, as fire is known by its heat, so the Unmanifest reveals Himself through the world of manifestation. The analysis of the substance of all created things, if carried sufficiently far, will lead to the discovery that what remains is identical and equally present in all creatures: it is He, it is That, which is styled as Pure Consciousness.

"If in the midst of the diversity of the world of appearances you make a sustained effort to do all your work as a faithful servant of the Almighty Father of the Universe, love and devotion for Him will awaken in your heart. As the confining prison walls of the ego are broken down, you will become more and more persistent and *wholehearted in your pursuit of Reality. Then all the manifold pictures you perceive will merge into one single picture and all your divergent moods and sentiments will be engulfed in the one great ocean of bliss.*

"The Universal Body of the Lord comprises all things – trees, flowers, leaves, hills, mountains, rivers, oceans, and so forth. A time will come, must come, when one actually perceives this all-pervading Universal Form of the One. The variety of His shapes and guises is infinite, uncountable, without end. Just as ice is nothing but water, so the Beloved is without form, without quality, and the question of manifestation does not arise. When this is realised, one has realised one's Self. For, to find the Beloved is to find my Self, to discover that God is my very own, wholly identical with myself, my innermost Self, the Self of my Self. First of all it is necessary to become acquainted with Him whom you wish to invoke. Constantly think and talk of Him, look at his pictures, sing His praises or listen to sacred music, visit places of pilgrimage, seek solitude or associate with the holy and wise, so as to become familiar with Him.

"When this has been achieved, you may call Him 'Father' or 'Mother'. Some relationship of this kind has to be established with Him, because people of the world do not feel affinity unless their bond is defined in such a manner. You are accustomed to ties of kinship in worldly life; this is why you have to bind yourself by some sort of relationship in the spiritual field as well. Even though at the start you may not feel deep devotion, learn to invoke Him unceasingly and with perseverance by repeating His name, or by

any other method, until gradually He will fill your heart. However, prayer, meditation, alms offered in His name, and so forth, are necessary even after the bond of love has been forged, so as to keep it unimpaired. In this way the awareness of Him will become your second nature and never leave you to your last breath. This is what is termed communion with God.

"Listen! Do not let your time pass idly. Either keep a rosary with you and do japa; or if this does not suit you, at least go on repeating the name of the Lord regularly and without interruption like the ticking of a clock. There are no rules or restrictions in this. Invoke Him by the name that appeals to you most, for as much time as you can — the longer the better. Even if you get tired or lose interest, administer the name to yourself like a medicine that has to be taken. In this way you will at some auspicious moment discover the rosary of the mind, and then you will continually hear within yourself the praises of the great Master, the Lord of Creation, like the never ceasing music of the boundless ocean; You will hear the land and the sea, the air and the heavens reverberate with the song of His glory. This is called the all-pervading Presence of His name.

"Silent japa should be engaged in at all times. One must not waste breath uselessly; whenever one has nothing special to do, one should silently practice japa in rhythm with one's breathing. In fact, this exercise should go on continually until doing japa has become as natural as breathing.

"It is of great value to read sacred texts and books of wisdom. Speak the truth. Bear in mind that God's name is He Himself

in one form; let it be your inseparable companion. Try your utmost
never to remain without Him. The more intense and continuous
your efforts to dwell in His presence, the greater will be the
likelihood of your growing joyful and serene. When your mind
becomes vacant, endeavour to fill it with the awareness of God
and His contemplation.

"The Supreme Father, Mother and Friend – verily God is all
of these. Consequently, how can there be a cause or reason for His
Grace? You are His, and in whatever way He may draw you to
Him, it is for the sake of revealing Himself to you. The desire to find
Him that awakens in man, who has instilled it into you? Who is it
that makes you work for its fulfillment? Thus you should try to arrive
at the understanding that everything originates from Him. Whatever
power, whatever skill you possess – why, even you yourself – from
where does everything arise? And does it not all have for purpose the
finding of Him, the destroying of the veil of ignorance? Whatever
exists has its origin in Him alone. So then, you must try to realise
your Self. Are you master even of a single breath? To whatever small
degree He makes you feel that you have freedom of action, if you
understand that this freedom has to be used to aspire after the
realisation of Him, it will be for your good. But if you regard yourself
as the doer and God as being far away, and if, owing to His
apparent remoteness, you work for the gratification of your desires,
it is wrong action. You should look upon all things as manifestations
of Him. When you recognise the existence of God, He will reveal
Himself to you as compassionate or gracious or merciful, in
accordance with your attitude towards Him at the time – just as,
for example, to the humble he becomes the Lord of the Humble.

"Through breath energy, consciousness pervades matter. Everything that is alive breathes. When breath stops, you die. Physical life depends on breath. Through prana, matter becomes alive. Desires and a wandering mind make the breath impure. Therefore, I advise the practice of concentration on breathing combined with taking any one of God's names. If the breath and the mind become one-pointed and steady, then the mind expands to infinity, and all phenomena are included in that one all-inclusive point. If you think of God with the breath it will purify the prana, the physical sheath and the mind. If you breathe while thinking of God's name, you will feel the call of His grace.

"The Self, or God, is unknowable to the ordinary intelligence, but He is not unknown to us as the life-breath. If one uses the rhythm of one's breathing as a support in meditation, this increases one's power. Therefore, one should daily sit in a meditative pose in a solitary place and turn the mind inward, and repeat the mantra in rhythm with one's breathing, without straining, in a natural way. When through prolonged practice, the name becomes inextricably linked with the breath, the body quite still, one will come to realise that the individual is part of the One Great Life that pervades the Universe."

MA'S GOOD WORK
CONTINUES

Many ashrams have been established in North India, under Ma's direction. When Ma's body was enshrined in the ashram at Kankhal, just south of the holy pilgrim town of Haridwar, the main centre of activities was moved from Varanasi to this ashram. Here, books and videos about Ma in many different languages are available and programmes are conducted throughout the year, including the continued observance of the Samyam Saptah. In large cities like Kolkota and Delhi, the ashrams have many guest rooms, large kirtan halls and *mandirs*. The Varanasi ashram, situated on the banks of the holy Ganga, houses the Kanyapeeth School for girls. The ashram also runs a large charitable hospital. There are some ashrams in the wilderness, such as the one built at the foothills of Almora, and the picturesque ashram in Bhimpura, Gujarat, sitting high on a hill overlooking the sacred Narmada River.

In the 1990s, two ashrams were established in Ma's name

in Madhya Pradesh by her disciple Swami Kedarnath. One ashram is in the city of Indore, and the other in the ancient and venerated pilgrim centre of Omkareshwar, on the banks of the Narmada river. The Omkareshwar ashram serves as a retreat centre for devotees wishing to spend quiet time in meditation in a serene and uplifting environment.

Swami Kedarnath has recently completed the monumental task of compiling all the recorded words of Ma handed down to us in transcribed conversations, dictated letters and questions and answers during satsangs, and has assembled them into a six-volume set entitled *Mata Anandamayi Vachanamrit* (The Immortal Teachings of Ma Anandamayi). He has arranged many of Ma's sayings by subject and enriched the text with his own profound commentary. After completing this task, he has analysed and scrutinised Ma's teachings to find recurrent themes, and has written two profound philosophical works based on Ma's views and teachings. These books, entitled *Purna Pragyapti Darshan* (The Vision of the Knowledge of Perfect Fullness) and *Ma Anandamayi Vedant* (The Philosophy of Unity of Anandamayi Ma) lend greater understanding to her teachings. These books are currently only available in Hindi, but are also being translated into English and other languages.

Ma says: *"I say to you that I am a little child and you are my parents. Accept me as such and give me a place in your hearts. By saying 'Mother', you keep me at a distance. Mothers have to be revered and respected. But a little girl needs to be loved and looked after, and is dear to the heart of everyone. So this is my only request to you: to make a place for me in your hearts!"*

NEW INCIDENTS COME
TO LIGHT

I spoke with one Brahmacharini who had been associated since her childhood with Ma, and whose father had been a very close devotee of Ma for many years. On one occasion, her father was present when Ma was invited to consecrate the images in a temple. A large crowd had gathered on this occasion and as the man was walking with Ma towards the shrine, she instructed him to hold on to the edge of her white *dhoti* so they would not get separated in the rush of the crowd. So, with him holding the end of Ma's dhoti, they entered the temple followed by a huge, jostling crowd. After Ma had performed the rites, and while he was still tightly holding on to the edge of the cloth, he glanced backwards at the huge mass of people jamming the hall and walkway of the temple and wondered how they would make their way back out to the gate. At that moment he felt a cool breeze blow through him, even ruffling his hair. This puzzled him, as it was very stuffy inside the temple with the huge crowd jamming it. He then looked down at his hands and found that he was no longer holding on to Ma's dhoti and she was nowhere to be seen. The next moment someone called out, "Look! Ma is back at the entrance of the walkway!" He looked far down the walkway towards the end of the crowd and saw Ma's radiant, white-robed figure standing calmly. He slowly made his way through the crowd and when he finally stood before her, she simply looked at him and laughed merrily.

Once, a certain family had fallen deeply into debt due to an unexpected tax levied against them by the authorities. The deadline had come for payment and they were being threatened with impending imprisonment. As they were despairing for their future, a man suddenly arrived at their door with a message and a bank draft from Ma's ashram that was located in a different province. The man explained that some devotees had come to the ashram and offered a large donation. On hearing of this, Ma (who had not been informed of the family's plight) had told them to take it to this family instead, giving them the address. When they examined the draft, they found it was made out for the exact amount that was needed to pay their debt.

I also happened to speak with a young man who told me his father had witnessed the following incident. On one occasion, he was sitting near Ma when he saw a large ant crawling on the seat she was sitting upon. Fearing that the ant might bite Ma, he reached forward and with great force slapped his palm upon the ant, crushing it mercilessly. Ma asked him why he had done such a cruel thing. She then gently picked up the dead ant and, placing it in the palm of her hand, looked at it tenderly for a moment. She then placed it back on the ground. The ant revived quickly and scurried off.

Once, a man approached Ma and asked for initiation with a sacred mantra. She told him that he should first write a certain Divine Name a specified number of times. She told him that he should write some every day and keep a count of it. Whenever he finished writing it, she would give him the initiation. The man set about his task systematically, writing the name every day in a notebook. At first he kept count but as time passed, he just wrote without keeping any count of how much of the task he had completed. After some months had passed, he happened to be visiting the ashram in Varanasi at a time when Ma also was visiting there. One morning after completing his writing of the sacred name in the notebook, he went for his meal in the ashram's dining hall. Just as he sat down, a message came for him, "Come quickly! Ma is calling you." He got up and made his way to Ma's room, where he found her happily waiting for him. She told him, *"Tomorrow you shall have your initiation. Prepare yourself."* Overjoyed, but somewhat perplexed at the suddenness of it all, he returned to his room. He then thought to check and count the number of times he had written the Divine Name. After checking all the notebooks he had filled, he found that without his being aware of it, he had finished the exact number specified by Ma. Even though he had lost count, Ma had not.

A great yogi and saint, whom I know personally, related to me that before coming to Ma he had spent decades in intense yogic and ascetic practices and although having reached exalted states, he felt he had not reached the final goal. He petitioned Ma for initiation and she appointed a certain time and took him alone into a private room. He said that as soon as Ma had closed the door, her entire body began to radiate a gentle light that lasted throughout the meeting. When he had sat down in front of her, she began to tell him without asking any questions, all that he had done to find God in this life, describing each specific sadhana he had practiced. He sat in mute astonishment, but Ma simply laughed sweetly. She then told him she would impart a mantra he had used in a previous birth, which would be very effective for his spiritual progress in this life.

In Didi Gurupriya's diaries, it is written that Ma did or said something while in the midst of many people that only Didi herself, or someone who was intended to hear or see, heard and experienced. This may seem puzzling, but as Ma was a realised Being and not confined within time and space, she seemed to do this quite often. I spoke with one Brahmacharini who said that when she was a teenager, she was once standing in line to offer pranam to Ma at the end of a satsang. At that time, Ma's health was quite poor and therefore her attendants were telling people not to touch her, and were forming a tight guard around her to prevent any contact as people made their obeisance before her. As the girl stood in line, she felt an intense longing to touch Ma's feet and she began mentally complaining to her about not being allowed to do so. As her turn came and she stood before Ma, she said that she suddenly found that 'time had stopped' and she was in a completely private world with Ma. Although they were in a noisy room, suddenly to her ears there was no sound and she saw only Ma, who then extended her feet and the girl knelt down and lovingly held them to her head in reverence. Then as she stood up, the noise returned to her ears. The attendants were there guarding Ma's person and she moved on, realising that no one else had seen that magical moment when she 'stole' the touch of Ma's feet.

In a similar incident, the wife of a devotee from London once received a mantra from Ma in a dream. This happened with many devotees of Ma. The mantra given in initiation is meant to be a secret between the guru and the disciple. The next time the woman came to see Ma in India, she related the dream and asked if this was a true experience. Ma affirmed that it was and confirmed the mantra that the woman had heard in her dream. Although there were several people in the room and she was sitting at some distance from Ma, on later enquiry she realised that although the entire conversation was heard by everyone present, the actual uttering of the mantra which they both spoke was heard by no one in the room except herself and Ma. She also related that while speaking the mantra, a bright light shone on Ma's face.

I myself had a similar experience. I was once sitting with Ma in Kanpur which is in Uttar Pradesh. There were perhaps a hundred people, all sitting with their eyes fixed on Ma, and I happened to be sitting very close to the small platform that

Ma was seated upon. Suddenly, Ma leaned over and placed her face directly in front of mine and looking into my eyes, spoke several sentences with great force and clarity that sounded to me like specific instructions. She spoke in Bengali and since I knew nothing of the language, I didn't understand any of the words that she said. After speaking the sentences in this manner, Ma sat back. I then turned to several Brahmacharinis who were standing by her and asked them what Ma had just said to me. They appeared somewhat puzzled by my question. After enquiring from several people who were present, I found to my amazement that no one in the crowd had seen Ma lean over and speak to me. As everyone else watched, Ma appeared to simply remain seated and looking in front of her. Only I saw her lean over and speak to me. This experience is imprinted on my mind, forever!

Recently, the following incidents were narrated to me directly by a very senior, scholarly and saintly devotee, who spent twenty-two years in close contact with Ma.

One day, this saintly devotee and his wife boarded a city bus in Pune to visit Ma at her ashram. Ma would usually respond to the sincere yearning of her devotees to see her by coming to meet them – sometimes in the most surprising ways! Looking out of the bus window, this couple was amazed to see Ma walking completely alone along the side of the road unaccompanied by any attendant, which was rare during the latter days in her life. After a few minutes, when the bus reached its next stop, they got down and hurried back up the road in the direction they had seen Ma walking. Reaching a crossroad, and not seeing Ma anywhere, the man noticed a signboard of a Christian convent a short distance ahead.

Intuitively feeling that this was where Ma had gone, the couple started towards the convent and upon reaching its gates, inquired if Anandamayi Ma had been there. They were directed to one of the principal staff members who told them that Ma had certainly come but had just left. He further confided that since he had heard that Ma was visiting Pune, he had been longing for her darshan but had been unable to go to her ashram. Suddenly, to his great surprise and joy, Ma came in through the door, greeted him and spoke warmly with him for several minutes. Asked where Ma had gone now, the man pointed in the direction of a small hut where a poor family of workers lived near the convent gate.

The couple entered the little hut only to find a scene of mourning over a death that had just occurred. They described Ma to the family and asked if she had been there. They were told that a lady meeting this description had come and mercifully placed her hands on the dying man's head and blessed him just minutes before he passed away, and then she had left. The couple made their way back to the ashram expecting to see Ma on the way, as they were following just minutes behind her. Upon reaching the ashram, they inquired of Ma's attendants as to when Ma had returned from outside. They were met with questioning glances and informed that they had been with Ma the entire day, and that she had never left the ashram. When they met Ma, she simply looked at them and smiled knowingly.

Ma asked this man and his wife to learn Sri Vidya – the meditations and worship connected with the Sri Yantra, the sacred geometric symbol of the Divine Mother. The fruition of this suggestion came about in a remarkable manner.

One day in the Vrindavan ashram, Ma asked the couple what the astrological conjunction was for the day and the hour. Not knowing the answer, the man went and brought Swami Satchidananda, a very learned *Danda Swami*, and the three of them sat before Ma. Upon knowing the exact astrological positions at that moment from Swamji, Ma exclaimed, *"This is a very auspicious moment,"* and then fell silent. After a few minutes, she raised her eyes upward and, to the astonishment of the three onlookers, turned completely red! Her skin, her hair, and even her immaculately white clothing turned a brilliant red* and remained so during the entire episode that followed. Next, Ma opened her mouth and a stream of Sanskrit mantras emanated rapidly with perfect articulation. While the intonation was going on, Swami Satchidananda leaned over and whispered to the man, "These are the mantras for Sri Vidya." After several minutes of rapid chanting, Ma again fell silent and her normal colour returned. She then instructed the couple to meet Swamiji the next morning and he would teach them the puja of Sri Yantra.

* Red is the colour associated with Tripura Sundari, the form of the Divine Mother represented in the Sri Yantra.

The next morning they met Swamiji in the ashram temple. He asked them if they remembered any of the mantras that Ma had recited spontaneously, as the ritual was complex and he felt that they should only learn the part that they remembered intuitively. They replied that all the mantras were new to them, and they couldn't remember a single one of them. When told to try and remember, they looked into each other's eyes and, suddenly, both husband and wife began to simultaneously recite the complete mantras that Ma had spoken. Swamiji simply smiled and said, "This is Ma's way of saying you should learn the entire puja."

This same couple were at another time sitting with Ma, when a sadhu entered the room and began to speak in a desperate and pleading voice. He told Ma that he had practised an advanced yoga kriya for years, but was unable to accomplish the next stage of the meditation that was required for his advancement. He had approached Sri Aurobindo of Pondicherry, considered to be the greatest yogi of India at the time, who had told him, "I am familiar with the kriya you practice, and I am aware of the state you have attained. I further know how to proceed but, unfortunately, neither I nor any other yogi can instruct you in this matter as this is an advanced practice. The only person living who can help you is Ma Anandamayi. Go to her."

So, the sadhu had made the long journey from south India to where Ma was staying. He repeatedly beseeched her to help him, but Ma simply replied, *"Fir se koshish karo"* – *"Try again."*

He began to weep and said imploringly, "Ma, if you refuse me, I have nowhere else to turn, and my spiritual progress which has reached such an advanced stage, will be forever stopped!" Hearing this, Ma sat silently for some time. Then raising her eyes, she made a dramatic, sweeping movement with both hands as if opening the heavens, and said loudly, *"Khol diya!"* – *"I have opened it!"* At the sound of these words, the man was drawn up erect like a statue and sat motionless for over an hour. Upon returning to outer consciousness, he fell at Ma's feet with tears of gratitude proclaiming that he had entered a deep state of samadhi which far exceeded any experience he had had so far and, in this state, he had all his questions answered and been taken to the next stage of his advancement.

Note: As stated earlier in this book, Ma's life can be written a thousand times over by countless devotees, all of whom experienced beautiful and intimate moments of Ma's guidance, care and love. I have included here a few incidents that, to my knowledge, have not been written about in any of the books published about Ma. I heard these incidents directly from the devotees themselves – all reliable people – and narrated one incident that I experienced myself.

Anyone who speaks with Ma's devotees can find endless stories like those mentioned above to illustrate Ma's care and concern for all those whom she called to her. Ma has become the shining beacon of enlightenment and the embodiment of the loving, maternal nature of God. Her immortal presence in the world transcends all barriers of sect, religion and lineage. She is the Mother of all and the joy and consolation of all who know of her.

MY MEMORIES
OF MA

I first came to Ma in 1973, after having lived for a year in an ashram established in Ma's name in America by an American sanyasi, Swami Nirmalananda, who had been closely associated with her for the past ten years. I had read and studied Ma's life, and faith in her had already begun to grow in my heart even before I actually set eyes on her.

I came to India with Swami Nirmalananda and three other *brahmacharis* from the ashram. At that time, Ma was staying in the beautiful garden-ashram in Vrindavan, the holy town of Lord Krishna. Arriving at the ashram, we enquired where Ma was and were taken to her room, which was in a small building, in a secluded corner of the forested ashram grounds. We were conducted into an outer sitting room and told that Ma had been in samadhi all morning, in the inner chamber, but they would try and convey to her that we had arrived.

I had pondered many times what it would be like to meet Ma, whom I had come to regard as a perfect manifestation of divinity. My imagination had conjured up scenes ranging from Hollywood movies complete with special dramatic effects, to scenes from the *Puranas* in which the deity descends from the heavens in a celestial chariot, adorned with diadems and multiple arms. Now I tried to simply sit quietly and calm my mind in anticipation of the experience.

After a few minutes, Ma emerged from the inner room and sat in front of us on a small, raised *asan*. She was clothed in spotless white and was the image of simplicity and gentleness. She appeared indrawn and for quite some time didn't speak at all, but simply sat serenely, looking sweetly at us all. My initial reaction was a feeling of quiet awe mixed, strangely, with a deep familiarity. This was someone I had known or experienced before, but I didn't know how or where. I saw no spectacular lights or visions, but a feeling of peace and security began to radiate from within my own heart. I felt as if I had come home and was meeting someone nearer and dearer to me than anyone else in the world.

For a long time, Ma simply looked directly and silently into the eyes of each of us. When her eyes met and held mine, I realised this was an experience that was totally and completely unique, something I had never experienced before. There was nothing in this world that could produce the feelings and perceptions that were arising in my mind, so I had no former basis to compare or comprehend these reactions. First of all,

I became aware of my own soul and saw myself as a spiritual being, rather than a physical entity. Ma's glance penetrated all the layers of mind and personality and looked directly at my true inner essence, allowing me also to suddenly wake up to this true existence within myself.

I knew from the depths of my mind that this was someone who had known me from eternity, and whom I was an integral part of and would never be separate from. The revelation was at once profound but, at the same time, so natural and integral to my being, that it somehow didn't overwhelm me. I realised: THIS is Reality, and the only thing Real in this entire fleeting world. From that moment I was Ma's and Ma's alone.

Every contact with Ma after this was an experience of sweetness and bliss. In the mornings, I would kneel before her and offer a flower garland, draping it around her knees. She would touch the garland to her head and place it around my neck with a sweet smile and pranam that filled me with unearthly joy.

I arranged to have a private interview with Ma. At that time, I didn't speak Hindi or Bengali, so one of the inmates of the ashram translated for me. I told Ma that I had come to her to beg for all that was required for my spiritual life. I wanted the divine mantra of the name of God, and the empowerment and guidance to further proceed in sadhana. I said that I wanted to live the life of a sadhu under her direction and realise God. She asked me several questions about my life and practice and assured me that all would happen at the appropriate time.

After the interview, I noticed that Swami Nirmalananda, who had been waiting outside, was watching Ma very closely as she walked on the verandah outside her room. He told me, "I have observed Ma for many years, and I can tell by her eyes and mannerisms that she is exceptionally happy this morning. She has told us, *'My food is dedicated souls'*, and I think that whatever transpired in that room between you has pleased her very much." This greatly encouraged me and gave me the solace that Ma had accepted me, even though she had said nothing specific about my initiation. At every later request, she simply replied, *"The right time will come."*

I found that there was great bliss in just watching Ma. Her simple movements and actions displayed a freedom, dignity and beauty that cannot be described in words, and filled the beholder with a strange, inexplicable joy. Every evening, everyone in the ashram would gather in the mandir for satsang and kirtan in her presence. We all felt that Ma was pouring her blessings on each one of us, and that we were no longer held within the sphere of earth, but were soaring in the rarefied realms of the highest heavens!

One evening during kirtan, Ma was striking a small pair of cymbals and swaying gracefully from side to side. I was sitting some distance away from her, and she would occasionally give me a brief, sidelong glance and a sweet smile. Sitting there in sacred Vrindavan, I experienced in these brief glances, what the *gopis* must have felt when they gazed on Lord Krishna. Each time her fleeting glance fell on me, it was as if she was pouring honey into my whole soul. It was a sweetness that was so rich and tangible, it actually felt like a physical substance. But at the same time, it was a joy and delight that was incomparable to anything that this ephemeral earth can provide.

One memorable morning, Ma had been giving darshan on the roof of her ashram and was just rising to go into her room. All the devotees longed for more time with Ma, and feeling their inner desire, Ma lingered at the door of her room, and began speaking to us once again. She began to speak very seriously about spiritual life and its accompanying obstacles and gave practical advice. The longer she spoke, the more animated she became, and the more powerful her words. We listened breathlessly. She even shocked people at one point by declaring forcefully, *"Anything or anyone who stands in the way of your spiritual progress should be ruthlessly abandoned. Simply take your foot and kick them out of your way!"* As she said these words, she demonstrated this action with her own foot, much to our delight. These words and actions left a deep impression on my mind, and have helped me many times when obstacles arose before me.

After many days, Ma sent word that the next morning she would initiate me, and left specific instructions as to the preparations that were needed and the articles I should bring. I suddenly realised that the next day was the actual day of my physical birth – my twentieth birthday. Years later, when I had my Vedic astrological chart read, I found that in the early part of my life I was under a negative and materialistic influence governed by the planet Venus. This ended at the very beginning of my twentieth year. Everything is right in Ma's time. Now every year I celebrate both my physical and spiritual birth on the same day.

Ma specifically forbade me to reveal the actual events of my initiation to anyone. However, I can describe one event of that morning. I was expecting that on the day of my initiation, the angels would sing over my head and shower flower petals from heaven. The reality of the occurrence was just the opposite. I came at the appointed time and sat in the area behind the mandir where a small altar had been erected, and everything was in readiness for the ritual. Swami Bhaskarananda told me that Ma would be in shortly, and that I should sit and meditate. Ma kept me waiting for over two hours, and during that period I experienced an inner cleansing and purification that was almost beyond my endurance to bear. Fortunately, she gave me the bare minimum amount of detached observation to be aware of what was happening, so that I wasn't swept away by the experience. My ego began screaming with an audible mental voice: 'Get out of here now, before it's too late! Run!.. return to America, get married, get a job and forget all this nonsense!' Every impurity, every doubt, every resistance to higher life poured from the depths of my mind with incredible intensity. After about two hours of this burning torment, during which I had to virtually hold on to the floor to keep from running out of the temple, my mind at last began to calm down and only then did Ma enter the room.

After the ritual, I returned to my room and sat to meditate. I experienced that every thought and movement of my mind and heart was moving in a circle, flowing out from me and entering into Ma, and then returning in a completed cycle back into me. I have felt this connection from that time, and it has continued to grow and develop as the years proceed. Later that day, I asked Ma for a new name as I felt I had received a new life and she gave me the name 'Matriprasad', which means 'Mother's Grace'.

From that time, I tried to stay close to Ma at all times. I travelled with her to many different ashrams whenever she allowed. During times when she disappeared from public gaze with just a few attendants, she would tell me to go to Haridwar on the banks of the Ganges and meditate as much as I could, joining her later at her next public function.

The first private session I had with Ma after my diksha began in an unusual way. There was a small group of westerners who had arranged for private interviews with Ma, and we were told that she would see us all on one particular evening. We waited outside the hall and went in one at a time. I found that as the people in front of me came out, they had all discussed worldly matters and ambitions with her: their family and marital problems, their aspirations for jobs etc., and were happy with the answers Ma had given. When my turn came, I went into the room and sat before Ma. But before I could say a word, Ma leaned over and placing her face directly in front of mine, asked me forcefully, *"Are you married?"* I replied, "No, Ma." Keeping her face directly in front of mine, she continued, *"Have you ever been married?"* I again answered, "No, Ma!" Then she sat up straight and with a beaming expression and smile said in great joy: *"Ahh! A brahmachari!"* Ma led everyone according to their need, but this marked preference for the dedicated life of spirituality registered deeply in my mind, and helped me in times that I had to choose which direction to move in. Several years later, I wrote a letter to Ma from America, and she specifically gave me the instruction, *"Live the life of a renunciate."* These two events shaped my whole life.

Some of the best times spent with Ma were in the small ashram in Naimisharanya, a secluded village near Lucknow. This ancient holy site, on the banks of the Gomti River, is where Rishi Vyas wrote the Puranas and hosted a huge gathering of rishis in ancient times. When I was there with Ma, there were only about a dozen people around, and we had beautiful and intimate satsangs with her at night. One night, while looking lovingly at us, she said, *"You must always be very careful about your life and actions, as you represent me now. You are my hands and my feet, and what people think of you, they think of me."* This incredible statement has come to my mind many times in making life's difficult decisions.

Once when travelling with Ma, I sat with her for several hours in the waiting room of a railway station, along with two attendants. I was sitting directly in front of her, and the whole time, her merciful gaze rested on me, with a look of maternal affection and grace that filled my heart. Occasionally, she asked me questions about my spiritual practice and gave some advice. Although I remembered the specific advice she gave about spiritual routine, meditation times etc., it didn't really apply until about twenty-five years later, when I was living in solitude in Omkareshwar, and thinking of how best to arrange my day in sadhana. Then I remembered Ma's words, and realised that she had been looking far into my future and giving me instructions that I could only then apply practically.

Once, I witnessed an event that might seem insignificant but had a wonderful charm to it. In the dead of night, we were waiting on a railroad platform in a small town in Uttar Pradesh. There was just a small group of us with Ma, and someone brought a chair out and placed it on the platform for Ma to sit on. I saw that sitting right next to the chair was a little village woman, squatting on her luggage. Ma leaned towards her and started a friendly conversation. I could follow enough to understand they were just discussing their destinations, the weather etc. but the lady was looking up at Ma with such love and joy, not knowing who she was, but experiencing a strange happiness she herself could not describe. After some time, one of the brahmacharis wanted to show Ma something, so a flashlight was brought and shone on the object in Ma's hand. The light illuminated Ma's face in the darkness of the night, and I saw the simple woman sitting close to Ma, staring up at her face with reverent awe. I thought to myself: 'Only in India, can one have a casual conversation with God while waiting for a train!'

On this very night, Ma worked a small but very practical miracle for me. With me was another American brahmachari, and though the rest of Ma's travelling party had reservations for the train, we had not been able to secure ours and faced the prospect of a long night sitting on our baggage in the aisle of a crowded train. As the train pulled in and slowly rolled past us, we observed that every compartment was packed and there was not a single empty berth. But when the train finally came to a halt, we saw that directly in front of us, in the crowded and overfilled compartment, were two empty upper berths being completely ignored by the other passengers. We quickly boarded the train and asked if the berths belonged to anyone. No one seemed to know, so we climbed up and passed the night in undisturbed sleep. It seems Ma had made reservations for us!

At Kanpur, a twenty-four hour kirtan of the *Mahamantra* was arranged. The chanting continued all day and night, and Ma often sat and watched as we all walked slowly around a beautifully decorated altar in the middle of the *pandal,* while chanting the kirtan to the accompaniment of drums and cymbals. At one point Ma got up and joined our group, walking and singing with us. Then, as we danced around her in a circle, she lifted her hands over her head and sang with us, increasing our fervour and bliss a thousand-fold.

Once in the ashram at Kankhal, I arrived in the morning to find Ma engaged in a wonderful game. Her arms were loaded with flower garlands, and she was pursuing all the inmates of the ashram, and garlanding them one by one. People were in humility objecting and saying, "Ma! How can YOU garland us?" But Ma continued in great joy and spirit. I stood watching the fun for some time, until Ma went back inside. Suddenly, she emerged all alone and walked directly over to where I stood. Then with great sweetness and love, she handed me a beautiful flower and smiled at me. I took the flower and fell at her feet, overwhelmed by the gentleness of her love.

When the new satsang hall of the Kankhal ashram was being consecrated, a small group of foreigners staying near Ma was not allowed inside, for fear of polluting the rituals, as we had no caste. As we stood outside the door and watched, feeling somewhat dejected, Ma left her seat and came out and spoke with us. She explained how these observances had to be honoured, and then told us to go across the road to the ashram kitchen and eat some *puris* that were being specially prepared for us. So we all went across and ate our fill and then returned to our place outside the hall. Ma again came out and talked and laughed with us, and asked each one of us just how many puris we had been able to eat. We all felt Ma's motherly love consoling us for not being allowed to enter into the joy of the ritual.

Although my intention was to remain in India for the rest of my life, and Ma had specifically blessed me for this once in a private interview, I didn't realise that this desire would not get fulfilled until many years later. After trying every possible way to get my visa renewed, I finally realised I would have to return to America. I had my last private interview with Ma in the Kankhal ashram. When I asked Ma if she had any further instructions, she simply replied, *"I have given the instruction. Simply follow it."* But after a brief pause, she told me with great force, *"Do japa of God's name at all times. Always do japa!"*

Shortly after this, I returned to America and continued my

sadhana in Swami Nirmalananda's ashram. I longed to return to Ma, but since I had left all my material possessions behind and offered my services to the ashram, I had to wait for my turn to return to India at the ashram's expense. Swamiji returned every year with one or two people from the ashram, but since I had spent so much time in India, others had preference over me for the chance to see Ma. In 1982, the news came that Ma had left her body and I realised I would never see that divine physical form again.

Circumstances finally arose when I could settle permanently in India, and Swami Bhaskarananda sent me to Ma's ashram in Omkareshwar on the banks of the holy Narmada river, where by Ma's grace my sadhana and *seva* continue. Though Ma's form is not to be seen in this world anymore, her guiding presence is felt in the hearts of all who turn to her in faith, and her revelation will come to anyone who truly calls out to her in love.

Through this small book, I have tried to give the reader some glimpses into the divine nature and life of Anandamayi Ma. It is my fervent hope that all who read it will in some way experience and receive her overwhelming love, guidance and blessing.

Note: On being initiated by Anandamayi Ma, I was given the name of Matriprasad. Much later, when I was initiated into Naishthhika Brahmacharya (monastic vows) by Swami Bhaskarananda, he gave me the name Mangalananda. A few years later, when I received sanyas diksha from Swami Kedarnath, he retained my name as Mangalananda and conferred the title of swami to my name.

ASHRAMS OF ANANDAMAYI MA

BIHAR

Rajgir,
Nalanda-803 116.
Tel: 06112-255362

DELHI

Kalkaji,
New Delhi-110 019.
Tel: 011-26826813

GUJARAT

Bhimpura, Chandod,
Vadodara-391 105.
Tel: 02663-233208

JHARKHAND

Near Bhatia Park,
Kadma,
Jamshedpur-831 005.

Main Road,
Ranchi-834 001.
Tel: 0651-2331181

MADHYA PRADESH

Bairagrarh,
Bhopal-462 030.
Tel: 0755-2641227

Mata Anandamayi Peeth,
18 A.B. Road,
Indore-452 001.
Tel: 0731-2524265

Mata Anandamayi Tapo Bhumi,
Sangam Parikrama Marg,
Omkareshwar-450 554.

MAHARASHTRA

Ganesh Khind Road,
Pune-411 007.
Tel: 020-25537835

ORISSA

Swargadwar,
Puri-752 001.
Tel: 06752-223258

Chandipur-Tarapeeth,
Bribhum-731 233.

TRIPURA

Palace Compound,
Agartala-799 001,
West Tripura.
Tel: 0381-220-8618

UTTAR PRADESH

Puran Mandir,
Naimisharanya,
Sitapur-261 402.
Tel: 05865-251369

Bhadaini,
Varanasi-221 001.
Tel: 0542-2310054

Ashtabhuja Hill,
Vindhyachal,
Mirzapur-231 307.
Tel: 05442-252343

Vrindavan,
Mathura-281 121.
Tel: 0565-2442024

UTTARAKHAND

Patal Devi,
Almora-263 602.
Tel: 05962-233120

#2, Dhaul-China,
Almora-263 881.
Tel: 05962-262013

Kankhal,
Haridwar-249 408.
Tel: 01334-246575

Near Himlok,
Kedarnath,
Chamoli-246 445.

Kali Mandir,
Uttarkashi-249 193.
Tel: 01374-224343

Kishenpur,
Dehradun-248 009.
Tel: 0135-2734271

#2, Kalyanvan,
176 Rajpur Road,
Dehradun-248 009.
Tel: 0135-2734471

#3, Raipur Ordinance Factory,
Dehradun-248 010.

WEST BENGAL

Agarpara, Kamarhati,
Kolkata-700 058.
Tel: 2553-1208

BANGLADESH

14 Siddheshwari Lane,
Ramna, Dhaka-17.
Tel: 0880-9356594

Kheora,
via Kasba,
Brahmanbaria-554.

GLOSSARY

Akhanda Brahmacharini or *Sanatan Kumari* – eternal and perpetual virgin

asan – dais

asanas – body postures in yoga

Atirudra Yajna – a religious rite for peace and the benefit of humanity

Bhaiji – revered brother

bhajans – devotional songs

bhav – spiritual emotion

bhava nadi – river of life

bhiksha – alms given to wandering monks

Bholanath – one of the many names of Shiva

brahmacharinis – celibate female aspirants

brahmacharis – celibate male spiritual aspirants; usually living in an ashram

Brahmacharya – celibacy

Brahmin – priestly caste of Hinduism, regarded as the 'highest' caste

Danda Swami – an honoured initiation of the Shankara tradition, in which a danda or staff is bestowed by a revered Acharya (teacher) of Danda Swamis

darshan – ritual viewing of a god or saintly person

devas – gods

Devi – goddess

Devi Bhagavati – divine goddess

dharma – path of righteousness

dhoti – flowing lower garment worn by Indian men; after leaving Bengal, Ma always wore this garment rather than the saree usually worn by women

Didi – elder sister

Didima – elder sister who is revered like a mother

diksha – ritual of initiation

Durga Puja – worship of goddess Durga

fakir – a Muslim holy man

gangajal – water from the Ganges river

Gayatri Mantra – a vedic chant to inspire righteous wisdom

ghee – clarified butter

ghunghat – veil drawn to cover the head and face with the loose end of a saree

gopis – milkmaids devoted to Lord Krishna

guru – spiritual teacher

Guru Diksha – initiation by a spiritual master

Hari – Vishnu, the supporter of the universe in Hindu trinity

ishta devta – the personal god to whom an individual prays

japa – chanting of a mantra

japa sadhana – daily practice of chanting mantras

Jyoti Peeth – centre of light

Kali Puja – worship of goddess Kali

karma – past action

kheyal – a passing thought, mood or frame of mind; Ma used the word to denote Divine Will manifesting through her speech and actions

kirtan – group singing of the names of God

kriyas – specific techniques of breathing in meditation

Kumbh Mela – great religious fair at which sadhus and Hindus gather from all over India *lila* – divine play

Ma – mother

Mahabhav – intense spiritual emotion resulting from oneness with God

Mahadeva and *Mahadevi* – Shiva and Shakti

Mahamantra – a powerful spiritual chant, "Hare Krishna, Hare Ram"

mahatmas – highly evolved persons

mandirs – temples

mantras – spiritual chants

Manusha Kali – the living, human form of Kali Devi

Mataji – revered mother

maun – complete silence

mridanga – clay drum used in devotional music

mudras – ways in which the fingers are joined and held together during ritual worship or classical dance

Namaaz – daily prayers performed by Muslims in the mosque

Narayana – one of the names of Lord Vishnu

Nawab – a Muslim noble

pandal – large ceremonial tent

pandits – learned Brahmins who have mastered sacred texts

pranam – form of greeting

prasad – sanctified food offering

Puranas – compilations of Hindu mythic tales of gods and goddesses

puris – round, fried, flour puffs

Purna Brahma Narayana – the fullness of God in human form

purnahuti – concluding offering to the sacred fire

Rakhi Purnima – the full moon night that falls on the festival of Rakhi

Ranga Didi – beautiful sister

Rishi – a sage who has experienced the realisation of Godhood

sadhakas – spiritual aspirants

sadhana – adoption of meditation, asceticism and devotional practices on the spiritual path *sadhana shakti* – divine power

sadhu – wandering holy man

samadhi – yogic inner trance

sampradaya – spiritual lineage

samskara – values of life; innate tendencies in the subconscious mind from previous births

Samyam Saptah – week of restraint

sanyas – renunciation; the final, formal state of monasticism

sanyasi – renunciate on the spiritual path; a member of the order of Swamis

saree – cotton or synthetic fabric wrapped and worn as an outer garment by Indian women

satsang – keeping company with a saint or devotees; spiritual gathering

Savitri Mahayajna – a yajna performed for goddess Savitri

seva – selfless service

Shaktas – worshippers of God as Mother

Shaligram – stones representing Lord Vishnu

Shankara – another name of Shiva

Shankaracharya – one of the five existing heads of the monastic order of India

shastras – holy scriptures or treatises on various subjects

sloka – Hindu chant

tapasya – ascetic discipline

Thakurma – grandmother

toli – group

Vedic – pertaining to the Vedas

vyakta rupa – visible embodiment

yajna – ceremonial rite

yantra – divinely-revealed geometric pattern associated with a mantra

yogasana – meditation posture

yogic – to do with yoga

For photos, books and more information
about Anandamayi Ma, visit: www.anandamayi.org

The Author may be contacted on email:
matriprasad@yahoo.com

For further details, contact:
Yogi Impressions Books Pvt. Ltd.
1711, Centre 1, World Trade Centre,
Cuffe Parade, Mumbai 400 005, India.

Fill in the Mailing List form on our website
and receive, via email, information on
books, authors, events and more.
Visit: www.yogiimpressions.com

Telephone: (022) 61541500, 61541541
Fax: (022) 61541542
E-mail: yogi@yogiimpressions.com

 Join us on Facebook:
www.facebook.com/yogiimpressions

Printed in Great Britain
by Amazon

13877339R00075